THE NAKED CHEF

THE NAKED CHEF

Jamie Oliver

MICHAEL JOSEPH · LONDON

For my family

MICHAEL JOSEPH

Published by the Penguin Group
Penguin Books Ltd, 27 Wrights Lane, London W8 5TZ, England
Penguin Putnam Inc., 375 Hudson Street, New York, New York 10014, USA
Penguin Books Australia Ltd, Ringwood, Victoria, Australia
Penguin Books Canada Ltd, 10 Alcorn Avenue, Toronto, Ontario, Canada M4V 3B2
Penguin Books (NZ) Ltd, Private Bag 102902, NSMC, Auckland, New Zealand

Penguin Books Ltd, Registered Offices: Harmondsworth, Middlesex, England

First published 1999
33

Copyright © Optomen Television and Jamie Oliver, 1999
Food photography copyright © Jean Cazals, 1999
Reportage photography copyright © David Eustace, 1999

The moral right of the author has been asserted

Typeset in 9/14pt ITC Officina Sans
Typeset by Rowland Phototypesetting Limited, Bury St Edmunds, Suffolk
Designed in QuarkXpress on an Apple Macintosh
Printed in Great Britain by Butler & Tanner Ltd, Frome and London

A CIP catalogue record for this book is available from the British Library

ISBN 0–718–14360–4

CONTENTS

INTRODUCTION

About the book

When I first moved to London I rented a tiny flat in Hampstead, with a kitchen the size of a cupboard. After that I moved to a Hammersmith basement flat which wasn't much better, so I knew only too well the restrictions of a small kitchen with only basic cooking equipment.

I had been cooking good food in a restaurant for some time, but found it difficult to re-create many of the recipes at home for lack of time, space, equipment or, sometimes, the availability to the average shopper of good-quality produce at reasonable prices. So, in an effort to re-create some exciting restaurant recipes in a limited kitchen, I found myself stripping down those recipes to something quite basic. I then adapted them, using what I did have in the cupboard, larder, fridge or garden.

Using this principle I have built up a foolproof repertoire of simple, delicious and feisty recipes. At the same time I have tried to avoid culinary jargon and any complicated, time-consuming process that isn't justified by the end result.

The aim of this book is to inspire you to get into the kitchen, fired with enthusiasm and confidence.

About me

I grew up in a pub in a small, pretty village called Clavering, near Saffron Walden in north Essex. Having lived there all my life, pulling pints, opening bottles of wine and cooking were all part of everyday life to me.

My interest in cooking began after I said to my dad one day, 'All my friends are getting pocket-money – can I have some, please?'

He smiled. 'No,' he said, 'but you can get up in the morning and *earn* some if you want!'

Dad always had a thing about getting up in the morning. I can clearly remember what used to happen if I overslept on a Saturday morning in the summer – he would be watering the window-boxes and would put the hose through my bedroom window and squirt me as my early morning call! Dad had a selection of pleasures awaiting me, all involving lots of hard work and generally a broom or a mop (I don't know who he shoved up the chimney, but luckily it wasn't me). After that I was 'promoted' to a spell in the wash-up, which was even harder and sweatier. I thought this was perhaps not macho enough for a cool and sophisticated eight-year-old – I decided that most of the hard-core action was in the kitchen with the real men, and that's where I wanted to be. Here my education began. And not only in the culinary department, because I also learnt some very choice language! I must have been a real pain for my dad's five chefs, but they were very patient and encouraging. This is where I began to learn my practical and technical skills.

I worked in the pub every Saturday and Sunday until I left school. When I was fifteen I had two weeks' work experience at the Starr at Great Dunmow, and Brian Jones and his head chef had enough faith in me during my second week there to put me in charge of a section. I was in my element, and this inspired my decision to cook for a living.

Fortunate enough to get a place at Westminster Catering College in Vincent Square, I commuted every day for three years. I was completely in awe of the enormous college and the cosmopolitan mix of students. It was wicked! I loved every single part of the course, not just the practical work, as there was always so much of interest going on throughout the college.

My personal taste for classy, modern food wasn't fully formed at this stage. As a young chef I naïvely thought that a busy plate was a good plate. It wasn't until I went to work at Château Tilques in France that I learnt that quality, real care, love and individual flair have to go into every stage of food preparation.

This was where my passion for food was conceived; surrounded by people who were so much more talented than I was, whose enthusiasm was highly contagious and very inspiring, I learnt all that I could.

The place to learn more, I thought, could only be London. Everyone in the restaurant scene was going mad for it; and I had to be a part of it.

I desperately wanted to learn about Italian food, and was lucky enough to get a job at Antonio Carluccio's Neal Street Restaurant, where their pasta and bread are undoubtedly some of the very best in London. Antonio Carluccio and his sidekick Gennaro are famous for their wonderful wild mushrooms. I thought it was so funny when, in the middle of the English porcini season, some old Italian men came to pick mushrooms for five days. They knew their stuff (quite important when you're picking mushrooms!) – they knew of 'secret' locations in the country, and returned each day with huge baskets of porcini. On Monday they looked extremely poor and scruffy but by Friday they were wearing really flashy new white top-of-the-range Nike trainers. Excellent! Picking mushrooms was obviously a well-paid job!

After a year at the Neal Street Restaurant, and finding that I loved Italian food, I felt I wanted an even broader knowledge of it. I then decided that I wanted to work at the River Café. I rang the restaurant at least ten times, attempting to speak to Ruth Rogers or Rose Gray to ask for an interview. Eventually I was able to speak to Rose – she sounded very cold and blunt; she scared the hell out of me! But I was soon to find out that it was just her telephone manner and that actually she is the nicest, warmest and most inspirational chef that I have ever met.

Nothing can prepare you for working at the River Café. It doesn't matter what you have learnt before – Rose Gray and Ruth Rogers's style is unique and unconventional, and it really works. For a chef, using the finest, freshest, organic produce and being involved in a new menu every session is the most exciting experience. Some of my recipes are inevitably inspired by what I learnt at the River Café, for I was always encouraged to use my imagination there. This is what I want to encourage in you . . . Go on, get stuck in!

FIRST MOVE

Whether you are just starting to cook, or you are an experienced cook having a surge of enthusiasm, the first things to consider are your commodities. When I was at college, one of our lecturers, Mr Hobbley, used to say to us every day, 'It's all about knowing your commodities!' over and over again. I used to mimic his voice a treat, but he was right. When you go shopping, have a look round your fancy shops and delis just to see what's going on. I can't afford stuff from Harrods and Selfridges but I just go in and look – it's great! There is a fantastic selection. It's a real education.

Commodities – sugars, flours, oils, herbs, mustards, vinegars . . . the list goes on and on, and any one, or any combination, can take a dish in a completely different direction. So get yourself some really good commodities, get some good olive oil, and you're half-way to a perfect dish.

Something like the following list could be the basis for some really exciting dishes. Then when you come home with a piece of meat or fish, some vegetables or some salad, there will always be something in the cupboard to give your meal a really nice touch.

- Mustards: Dijon, wholegrain, English
- Oils: extra virgin olive, olive, sunflower
- Vinegars: red wine, white wine, balsamic, rice wine
- Flour: plain, self-raising, strong pasta (fine strong) Tipo '00', corn
- Semolina, couscous
- Baking powder, bicarbonate of soda
- Sugar: brown, white, icing
- Salt: Maldon sea, table, cooking
- Dried pasta: spaghetti, linguine, tagliatelle, penne, farfalle
- Pulses: borlotti beans, cannellini beans, black-eyed beans, butter beans, yellow split peas, lentils, chickpeas
- Tinned tomatoes
- Rice: basmati, Arborio, Carnaroli
- Olives: black, green
- Nuts: pine nuts, whole almonds, hazelnuts
- Dried mushrooms: porcini
- Sun-dried tomatoes
- Chocolate: good-quality cooking (70% cocoa solids)
- Cocoa powder (70% chocolate)
- Soya sauce, fish sauce, oyster sauce
- Anchovies in olive oil or salt
- Capers: salted (small ones are best)
- Herbs and spices (see page 11)

HERBS AND SPICES

Fresh herbs

Fresh herbs are a must – you can use them in nearly every dish you make. They are so easy to grow in this country; whether you live in the city or the country, whether you're rich or poor, whether you live on the sixteenth floor or in a basement flat, it doesn't matter! Just stick them in your garden, window-box, terracotta pot, bucket – anything that doesn't move!

You must grow rosemary, thyme, sage and bay. They grow all year round outside, in rain, wind and snow, and can be picked all year. You don't have to do anything to them except water and feed them if they are in pots. They just get bigger. It's brilliant being able to pick sage for your stuffing on Christmas Day. Mint, oregano and marjoram can also be left in all year, but do die down in winter if they are not in a sheltered position. They always come back in the spring with a vengeance.

Some of the less hardy herbs such as basil and coriander can be grown successfully indoors on the window-sill. A friend of mine has a great big plant of purple basil in her kitchen; it looks brilliant. We can't keep buying those small packets of fresh herbs from the supermarket. Quite often we are paying high prices for substandard herbs, and not much of them either. And, without wanting to go on too much, the idea is that fresh herbs are to be picked and used in cooking for a really natural, fresh perfume, not sweating and wilting in plastic. So, let's sort it out!

Dried herbs

These do have their uses. They aren't the same as fresh herbs, and you must remember not to use as much because the drying concentrates the flavour. I actually think that oregano and marjoram are more useful when dried, because their flavours become more pronounced.

Spices

Spices are great. They are non-perishable, and just sit there waiting to be used. It's always cheaper to buy your spices loose or as refills, rather than in those small jars, but you should keep them in airtight containers.

The spices I keep in my larder as part of the basic commodities list on page 9 are:

- Black peppercorns
- Dried chillies
- Nutmeg
- Cloves
- Coriander seeds
- Fennel seeds
- Cumin seeds
- Caraway seeds

The pestle and mortar

This is probably the best investment you can make in the kitchen. Once you've got your herbs and spices sorted, the one thing that you *really, really* want is a pestle and mortar. I just couldn't do without mine. But don't go buying those small clay or porcelain ones, they are not really man enough for the job; get a chunky stone one. They don't crack or break and will last a lifetime (you can get them in Thai food shops for about £20).

Good soups are really only about good ingredients. A good soup can be made, finished and in a bowl in minutes and still be as tasty as one that you have spent an hour or so preparing. Soups are one of those things that anyone can make. It can be as simple as sweating off some fragrant vegetables, adding an additional flavour and a little stock, and that's it. Then you just have to choose whether you want to leave your soup chunky and brothy or purée it like baby food (after all, we all like baby food, don't we?). To make it different you can add some cream or some croûtons.

The good thing is that you can make soups out of just about anything, and with a little bit of thought they can be delicious. Whenever I make a soup I always make it for 4 or 6, even if it is just for me, and freeze the extra in those little plastic sandwich bags. (Freezing doesn't do the soup any favours but it will still be tastier than anything you can buy in a shop.)

Here are five of my favourite soups.

My Minestrone Soup

If you've tasted a real minestrone you'll understand what it's all about. There are many excellent minestrones in Italy, but from place to place and region to region they'll never be the same. There's not one recipe that embraces the whole idea of minestrone. The ingredients change with the seasons. In winter, when it's cold, you want the soup to be warming and filling, with more pasta and vegetables. In summer, when it's hot, you want a lighter, less substantial soup with things like baby asparagus, peas, broad beans, artichokes. At the River Café, in the summer, they make an amazing minestrone with mint and basil.

Little tips before you start

- I think it is nice to use a couple of different types of cabbage, such as savoy, curly kale, spring cabbage and even cavalo nero (black cabbage), which is available now at Sainsbury's and other good greengrocers.
- You can make this really special by making your own pasta (see page 44). Just roll out a thin sheet and slash it roughly and repeatedly with a knife until the pieces are the size you want. Your pasta should be irregular-shaped, looking nice and rustic! Blanch it quickly to remove excess flour (30 seconds only), then add to the soup when it is nearly ready.
- If you are using dried spaghetti, roll it up in a tea-towel. Then, holding both ends, run it down the edge of the table (which will break the spaghetti into little pieces).
- This soup is best made with gammon or ham stock, for example the stock left over after cooking a piece of boiled bacon (see page 131). Chicken or vegetable stock are fine, but add a little sliced pancetta or smoked bacon when you fry the vegetables and rosemary. Remember that gammon stock tends to be slightly salty, so check before you add any seasoning.
- Perfectly ripe fresh tomatoes are ideal, although good-quality tinned Italian tomatoes can produce an equally good result.

Serves 6

10 large ripe plum tomatoes (or 2 × 400g/14oz tins of
  tomatoes without the juice)
3 medium carrots
2 medium leeks
5 sticks of celery
2 red onions
1 cabbage (or equivalent mixture)
1 tablespoon olive oil
2 cloves of garlic, finely sliced
1 heaped tablespoon chopped fresh rosemary
850ml/1½ pints gammon or ham stock (or chicken or
  vegetable stock)
3 good handfuls of fresh basil
170g/6oz spaghetti (or ½ pasta recipe, see page 44)
salt and freshly ground black pepper
extra virgin olive oil
Parmesan cheese, grated

Score the tomatoes and place briefly in boiling water. Then skin, deseed and roughly dice. Peel or scrape the carrots, quarter lengthwise and chop. Remove the outer leaves of the leeks, quarter lengthwise, wash well and chop. Peel the celery with a peeler to remove the stringy bits, then cut in half lengthwise and chop. You can use celery hearts, which I love in salads, but minestrone is really meant for using up those outer sticks which we are not so enthusiastic about. Peel and chop the onions. When you are chopping all these vegetables, try to make them more or less the same size (around 1cm dice), but don't be too fussy; you won't find the Italians cutting equal-sized mini-dice, that just isn't home cooking. Wash and roughly chop the cabbage.

Put the olive oil into a warmed, thick-bottomed pan and sweat the carrots, leeks, celery, onion, garlic and rosemary over a medium heat until just tender (about 15 minutes). Add the chopped tomatoes and cook for 1–2 minutes. Add the stock, bring to the boil and simmer for 15 minutes, skimming if necessary. Add the cabbage, cover the pan and simmer for 10 minutes, then add the ripped up basil and the pasta, which will absorb the flavours of the soup. Simmer for a further 5 minutes or more. Taste and season. The soup should be quite thick, full in flavour, and the cabbage shouldn't be overcooked – you want to retain its deep colour.

Serve with some good peppery extra virgin olive oil and fresh Parmesan.

Creamy Aubergine, Cannellini Bean and Ricotta Soup

Serves 6
285g/10oz cannellini beans, soaked overnight
4 large aubergines
1 tablespoon olive oil
2 cloves of garlic, finely chopped
1–2 small dried red chillies, crushed or chopped
1 tablespoon chopped fresh basil
1 tablespoon chopped fresh parsley
565ml/1 pint chicken or vegetable stock (see page 223)
255g/9oz fresh ricotta cheese
salt and freshly ground black pepper
extra virgin olive oil

Rinse the soaked cannellini beans. Cover with water, bring to the boil, and simmer for about 1 hour or until tender.

Prick the aubergines with a knife, lay them on a baking tray, and bake them whole in the oven at its highest temperature for about 40 minutes.

Heat the olive oil in a deep pan and fry the garlic, chilli, basil and parsley until the garlic is softened but not coloured. Cut the baked aubergines in half and scrape all the sweet-smelling insides into the pan. Add the cooked beans and the stock. Bring to the boil and simmer for 20 minutes. Remove half the soup, purée it and return it to the pot. Stir it and season well. It should be creamy, gutsy and reasonably thick. Then stir in your lightly seasoned, broken-up ricotta.

Drizzle each bowl with some really good peppery extra virgin olive oil as you serve it, and eat with some warm fresh crusty bread.

Chickpea and Leek Soup

This is a recipe that my Aussie friend Bender found in some old recipe book. It is quick and easy to make and it tastes fantastic. The chickpeas go really creamy and moreish and the leeks go silky and sweet. These are just two simple flavours, and even though I'm a bit of a fresh herbs boy, this lovely light soup is very tasty.

Serves 6
340g/12oz chickpeas, soaked overnight
1 medium potato, peeled
5 medium leeks
1 tablespoon olive oil
knob of butter
2 cloves of garlic, finely sliced
salt and freshly ground black pepper
850ml/1½ pints chicken or vegetable stock (see page 223)
Parmesan cheese, grated
extra virgin olive oil

Rinse the soaked chickpeas, cover with water, and cook with the potato (see 'How to Cook Pulses', p. 157) until tender. Remove the outer skin of the leeks, slice lengthways from the root up, wash carefully and slice finely.

Warm a thick-bottomed pan, and add the tablespoon of oil and the knob of butter. Add the leeks and garlic to the pan, and sweat gently with a good pinch of salt until tender and sweet. Add the drained chickpeas and potato and cook for 1 minute. Add about two-thirds of the stock and simmer for 15 minutes.

Now decide if you want to purée the soup in some sort of processor, or leave it chunky and brothy, or do what I do which is purée half and leave the other half whole – this gives a lovely smooth comforting feel but also keeps a bit of texture. Now add enough of the remaining stock to achieve the consistency you like. Check for seasoning, and add Parmesan to taste to round off the flavours.

This is classy enough for a starter, but I like it best for lunch in a big bowl with a good drizzle of my best peppery extra virgin olive oil, a grinding of black pepper and an extra sprinkling of Parmesan.

Fresh Tomato and Sweet Chilli Pepper Soup with Smashed Basil and Olive Oil

I like this soup hot, but it can be served cold in summer. It looks nice, and the flavours work well together but still remain individual in taste. It goes well with a toasted sandwich of mozzarella, or some other creamy cheese, for lunch.

Serves 6
15 ripe plum tomatoes
3 medium red peppers
approx. 7 tablespoons extra virgin olive oil
1 tablespoon chopped fresh deseeded red chilli
salt and freshly ground black pepper
1 clove of garlic, finely chopped
2 tablespoons red wine vinegar, or to taste
565ml/1 pint chicken or vegetable stock (see page 223)
2 good handfuls of fresh basil leaves

Score the tops of the tomatoes, blanch in boiling water for about 20 seconds, or until you can remove the skins and deseed. Grill the peppers whole (to achieve a really sweet pepper taste they should be grilled until black), rest in a covered bowl, then peel and finely chop them.

Put the chopped peppers in a warmed, thick-bottomed pan with 2 table-spoons of extra virgin olive oil and the chopped red chilli. Add a pinch of salt and fry slowly for about 5 minutes. Add the chopped garlic and cook for a further 2 minutes. Then add the roughly chopped tomatoes and cook for about 10 minutes with another pinch of salt and the red wine vinegar so that they sort of melt and infuse themselves together. Add the stock and simmer for 15 minutes. Season to taste.

In a pestle and mortar (or a food processor) smash the basil to a pulp with a pinch of salt. Stir in the remaining olive oil and a drop more red wine vinegar. Drizzle the mixture generously over your soup.

Quite frankly these broths really get me going. When I first started making them I knew absolutely nothing about any sort of fusion or Asian-type food and I must admit I'm still not an expert. But that is not always the most important thing – get into the feel of things, try to work out for yourself what it's all about. A good broth isn't designed to fill you up on a cold winter's day, like a European soup; it should be light, refreshing, cleansing and almost therapeutic. It's all about simplicity. What I do is have a little mooch around the supermarkets checking out all the Far Eastern imported commodities, they're great and there are loads of them. My broths are inspired by what I can find and what I think is right.

The nice thing is that you can really pig out on broths. Make yourself a huge bowl of broth for lunch, filled with noodles, vegetables or whatever – it will be really good for you. (I don't suggest that you eat this kind of broth if you're on a first date, because if you eat it properly it includes a lot of slurping, sucking and all sorts of other things. You generally get whipped around the chops with a couple of noodles and will splat a load of broth over your face, so leave it a couple of weeks into the relationship!)

I'm going to give you two of my favourite recipes, but the idea is that you make up your own, using three or four components such as noodles, herbs, meat, fish or vegetables. Just remember, the most important thing is the broth itself. I like it to be clear with a good flavour (to clarify stock, see page 226).

When you serve fusion broths try serving the stock separate from the rest of the dish – it looks far more charming and special. Divide all the ingredients apart from the stock into serving bowls, then serve your boiling stock at the table from one of those Bodem teapots (or a regular teapot or jug will do). Add a big handful of fresh herbs to the stock – they will infuse their flavour like teabags. Simply pour the steaming stock over the vegetables and/or meat in each bowl and squeeze a little lemon juice over the top.

Dry Grilled Chicken with Ginger, Chinese Greens and Noodles in a Herb Broth

Serves 4
4 chicken breasts
salt and freshly ground black pepper
1 litre/2 pints chicken stock (see page 223)
1 heaped tablespoon fresh ginger, finely sliced
1 clove of garlic, sliced
300–400g/11–14oz Chinese greens (pak choy, Chinese broccoli, gai larn)
455g/1lb noodles
1 or 2 medium/large fresh red chillies, deseeded and finely sliced
1 handful of fresh coriander, torn
4 tablespoons soya sauce
1 lemon or lime

Bone and skin the chicken breasts, trimming off any excess fat. Season with salt. Get a griddle pan very hot, add the chicken breasts and cook on both sides until done. Remove to a board and allow to rest for 3 minutes, then slice at an angle, around 1cm apart. At the same time bring the chicken stock and ginger and garlic to the boil, then reduce to a simmer. I like to steam my Chinese greens above the stock until tender, or in the broth if you prefer.

While the stock is simmering, cook the noodles in boiling, salted water, drain, and divide between 4 deep broth bowls. Divide the greens among the noodles. Then place the cooked chicken slices on top, and sprinkle with the chilli, coriander and soya sauce. Finally, check the seasoning of the broth and then pour it over each bowl (you could serve it at the table, as mentioned in the introduction). Finish with a squeeze of lemon or lime juice.

Broth of Steaming Scallops, Prawns and Clams with Noodles, Black Beans, Coriander and Lime

Serves 4

170g/6oz black beans, soaked overnight
1 litre/2 pints chicken or fish stock (see page 224)
2 heaped tablespoons finely sliced ginger
8 medium scallops, trimmed, with roe on or off
8–12 raw tiger prawns, peeled, with dark intestinal vein removed
455g/1lb live clams
455g/1lb noodles
1 handful of fresh parsley or basil
2 good handfuls of fresh coriander
2 medium/large fresh red chillies, deseeded and finely sliced
salt and freshly ground black pepper
2 limes

Rinse the soaked black beans. Cover with water, bring to the boil, and simmer until tender. Bring the stock to the boil and simmer with the ginger. Steam the seafood above the simmering stock (if you don't have a steamer, place the seafood into a foil envelope, add a swig of water or white wine, and bake in the oven at its highest temperature for 5–10 minutes or until the clams open up).

While your seafood is steaming, cook the noodles in boiling salted water until tender and drain. Divide the noodles between 4 deep broth bowls and scatter with the seafood, beans, herbs and chilli. Check the seasoning of the broth and serve it from a teapot at the table. Finish with a squeeze of lime juice.

SALADS AND
DRESSINGS

For years salads have been very badly represented in this country, which I think is a shame because I really love them! So, let's try to excite you into attempting something a bit different. Most people can't get any enthusiasm for a limp and uninteresting salad, so chuck out your tasteless iceberg lettuce and your water-based dressings – and remember, green leaves are really good for you, so do yourself a favour and try to make salad a regular thing. Here's a selection of pukka salads and dressings that are so quick and simple you can't not try them.

Always make your dressings with really good olive oil. At the end of the day you get what you pay for with olive oil, there are no bargains! Your salad should be dressed just before its arrival at the table or else it'll be horribly soggy. Remember that salad dressings always taste better if you can make them just before you use them, though it's not the end of the world if you make a larger quantity and refrigerate it.

Root Salad

This is one of the nicest salads you can make. It's crunchy, tasty and really nice served with cheese (especially mozzarella and ricotta).

You need equal quantities of carrots (preferably baby ones), fennel and celery. To start with, wash the carrots and slice them into 10cm/4 inch lengths. The idea is to slice them as thinly as possible (it's easier if you cut down one side and then turn the carrot on to the flat edge). Trim off the bottom and the top stalks of the fennel bulb, pull away the slightly tougher outside leaves, then cut in half and slice as thinly as possible from the root up to the top.

Trim off the bottom of the celery and pull off the tough outside sticks. (I always peel celery with a peeler to remove the stringy bits and save them for things like stews.) For this particular salad you just use the bottom 10cm/4 inches of the celery including the root. This tastes and looks completely different from the rest of the celery – it's white, much more tasty and completely unstringy. Slice this in half, the same way as the fennel, and slice from the root to the top as thinly as possible.

Add some herb and red wine vinegar dressing (see page 42) and mix thoroughly. This is probably the only salad that I dress a few minutes before eating – giving the flavours slightly longer to infuse seems to benefit the salad.

Beetroot Salad with Marjoram and Balsamic Vinegar Dressing

Try to get fresh raw beetroot, preferably baby ones of similar size (if you can't get raw beetroot, pre-cooked is all right, but I don't particularly like it). Boil the beetroot in salty water until tender (you should be able to push the skin away easily with your thumb). Drain and cool slightly. Peel all the skin away with your fingers, pulling off the stalk. If the beetroot are quite small, just chop them in half or leave them whole; cut larger ones into quarters.

While still warm, dress the beetroot salad with marjoram and balsamic vinegar dressing (see page 42). This is really nice served at room temperature either on its own as a salad or with grilled or roasted fish.

Potato Salad

Start with about 455g/1lb of potatoes (it's important to use evenly-sized new potatoes, and you can either scrape them or peel them). Cook the potatoes in salted boiling water. Try to cook these perfectly so that they just fall off the blade of a knife when you stick it into the potato (you don't want the potatoes raw but you certainly don't want them falling apart either). As soon as the potatoes are cooked, drain them and put them into a bowl. It is very important to add your dressing at this stage, while the potatoes are still steaming hot (by allowing them to cool down in the dressing the flavours penetrate the potatoes). Here are three dressings that I like to use:

Potato salad with salsa verde

All you do is dress the potatoes with 2 large tablespoonfuls of salsa verde (see page 233).

Potato salad with olive oil, lemon and dill

Use olive oil and lemon juice dressing (see page 42) and add some roughly chopped fresh dill and a little salt and freshly ground black pepper. (Instead of dill you could try fresh mint, fresh parsley or fennel tops – they'll all work.)

Potato salad with dandelion and shallot

Again, use olive oil and lemon juice dressing (see page 42), add some thoroughly washed and roughly chopped dandelion leaves and some finely chopped shallot, and season to taste with salt and freshly ground black pepper.

Potato salad with salsa verde

Mixed Salad with Roast Tomatoes

Get some really gutsy and interesting things in here, it could be a mixture of anything – cos, radicchio, gem, radishes, fennel, celery. Add some fresh herbs, such as marjoram, basil or parsley. Once you've got all that together, put in some roast tomatoes, just to give the salad a bit of an edge. Try to pick perfectly ripe plum or cherry tomatoes – leave them whole if they are small, otherwise halve them – and put them into a bowl. Add a little chopped garlic, some chopped fresh thyme, a little chopped fresh basil, some dried oregano, which is brilliant, a little lug of olive oil, plenty of salt and freshly ground black pepper, and a touch of dried chilli (fresh chilli is nice too). Put the contents of the bowl into a roasting tray and roast really quickly, just to colour them up and sort of dry them out – it normally takes about 15 minutes in a very hot oven. Allow to cool. When your salad is ready to be eaten, dress it with olive oil and lemon juice dressing (see page 42) and scatter the roasted tomatoes over the top.

The Real Tomato Salad

When you buy red tomatoes don't just buy the ones that are in nice packets – check them, smell them. The perfect tomato should be deep red in colour and soft but not squashy. You can get some lovely cherry, yellow and tiger skin tomatoes in the supermarkets these days, and they can also be used to make this salad.

Slice the tomatoes up as thin as you like and lay them out flat on a large plate. Finely chop a *very small amount* of garlic (it's only a gesture as it is quite strong) and finely chop a *small amount* of shallot or red onion. Scatter the garlic and onions over the tomatoes. Sprinkle the salad with sea salt, and freshly ground black pepper and dried oregano. Scatter with some torn basil leaves and drizzle with balsamic vinegar and lots of extra virgin olive oil.

Radish and Fennel Salad

Radish and Fennel Salad

The quantities of this salad are really up to you, but I look for roughly two parts fennel to one part radish. When buying radishes look for those that are really firm. The longer, oval-shaped ones are really nice. Wash them and slice thinly. Fennel comes in two types: the thinner fennel and a rounder, fatter variety. It is the rounder, fatter fennel bulbs that you want – these are normally much more well packed, less stringy and generally have a lot more of the green tops, which you need.

Cut the tops and the excess stalk off the top of the fennel and set aside. Trim the bottom of the bulb and take away the outside leaves if they seem a bit tough. Cut the bulb in half and slice as thinly as possible from the root to the top. Put the radishes and the fennel into a bowl and cover with cold water, adding some ice. Leave for at least 15 minutes to get the radishes and fennel really, really crispy. Drain, spin them or pat them dry, put into a bowl and dress with olive oil and lemon juice dressing (see page 42). Chop the fennel tops and sprinkle them on top. This is great with grilled fish.

Endive Salad with Anchovy and Caper Dressing

I was given endive every day for my staff meals when I worked in France. It was in, on and beside every bloomin' meal I had. It was served raw with no dressing, so it was bitter and revolting. After that experience I hated it. I have since learnt that the bitterness of endive really works if cooked or dressed using flavours with real guts – anchovies and lemon are a perfect example. I think this salad is a really classy one – great as a starter.

You need 4 medium, good-looking endives (no brown leaves). Cut each one in half from the root to the tip, then into quarters and finally into eighths. Wash in cold water and drain, then pat or spin dry. Using a pestle and mortar smash up 6 fillets of anchovy and 1 tablespoon of capers (or you can very, very finely chop them). Put the mixture into a bowl and add olive oil and lemon juice dressing (see page 42 – but you won't want any salt in the dressing for this one because of the salt in the anchovies and the capers). Mix thoroughly, then add the endive. You may need a little extra lemon juice to taste.

Globe Artichoke and Celery Heart Salad with Parmesan, Lemon and Olive Oil

I first had this salad in a café in Italy. The presentation was rather dull but the taste was fantastic! The crispness of the raw celery and artichoke works perfectly with the olive oil and the lemon juice. It's really refreshing, and the richness of the Parmesan shavings pulls it all together. Nice!

Prepare 2 artichokes (see page 137), and slice them from root to top as thinly as possible. Take off the tough, stringy outside sticks from a head of celery – use the bottom 10cm/4 inches in the salad and save the rest of the celery for other cooking uses such as stews. Cut the celery in half and then slice as thinly as possible from the root to the top, saving any yellow leaves (the green leaves are bitter and horrible). Put the artichokes and celery into a bowl and season slightly with a little salt. Add the olive oil and lemon juice dressing (see page 42). Then, using a peeler, shave long strips of Parmesan over the top and sprinkle the salad with some of the roughly chopped yellow celery leaves.

Taste the salad – you may want a little extra lemon juice because that's what makes it work.

Warm Salad of Radicchio, Gem and Pancetta

Use equal quantities of gem lettuce and radicchio. Trim off the bottoms and remove the outside leaves, which aren't so good. Cut the gem and radicchio in half, then, remembering that it is actually the white root that is going to hold these leaves together, cut each half from the centre of the root out, roughly making 1cm wedges held together by a little piece of root. Gently wash in cold water, drain, spin or dry, and place in a bowl.

Fry some slices or lardons of pancetta or streaky bacon until golden and crisp. Dress the salad with either olive oil and lemon juice dressing or herb and red wine vinegar dressing (see page 42). Remove the pancetta from the pan with a slotted spoon and scatter over the salad.

*Globe Artichoke and Celery Heart Salad
with Parmesan, Lemon and Olive Oil*

Baby Spinach, Fresh Pea
and Feta Cheese Salad

Baby Spinach, Fresh Pea and Feta Cheese Salad

You need 2 large handfuls of baby spinach – check for nasty stalky or wilted bits and then give it a really good wash (nobody likes gritty spinach). Spin dry, and add to a salad bowl with 2 smaller handfuls of fresh peas (unless you are lucky enough to get young peas which are sweet and tender, you should blanch the peas in boiling, unsalted water and leave to cool). Dress the salad at the last minute with olive oil and lemon juice dressing (see page 42) and sprinkle crumbled feta cheese over the top.

Broad Bean, Asparagus and French Bean Salad with Mustard Dressing

For this salad you need equal quantities of broad beans, asparagus and French beans. Having podded all your broad beans, grade them: the smallest ones can be eaten raw and the larger ones need to be lightly blanched. If you have some larger broad beans that have tougher skins, place them in a pan of boiling water that *hasn't* been salted (salt will make the skins tough). If you feel that the skins are a little bit tough, simply remove them after blanching. Trim the base of the asparagus (try to pick out the baby ones) and, using a peeler, peel from below the tip to the bottom. Line up the french beans and remove the stalky ends, leaving the wispy tail ends on.

Boil the French beans until tender and do the same with the asparagus. Dress the salad with mustard dressing (see page 43), preferably while the asparagus and the beans are still hot.

Green Salad

I like to include rocket, watercress, baby spinach, some ripped up cos, mustard leaf, mustard cress and thinly sliced fennel. Just two, three or all of these things will give you a really interesting salad. Dress it at the last minute with marjoram and balsamic vinegar dressing, olive oil and lemon juice dressing or some herb and red wine vinegar dressing (see page 42).

Herb and Red Wine Vinegar Dressing

Serves 4

2 tablespoons red wine vinegar

5 tablespoons best olive oil

1 level teaspoon salt

1 level teaspoon freshly ground black pepper

1 heaped tablespoon chopped fresh marjoram

1 heaped tablespoon chopped fresh basil

1 heaped tablespoon chopped fresh parsley

3 tablespoons finely chopped shallots

Mix together all the ingredients, adding the shallots last.

Olive Oil and Lemon Juice Dressing

Serves 4

2 tablespoons lemon juice

5 tablespoons olive oil

1 level teaspoon salt

1 level teaspoon freshly ground black pepper

Mix together all the ingredients.

Marjoram and Balsamic Vinegar Dressing

Serves 4

2 tablespoons balsamic vinegar (just 1 tablespoon may be enough if it is a very good vinegar)

5 tablespoons olive oil

1 teaspoon freshly ground black pepper

3 heaped tablespoons chopped fresh marjoram

Mix together all the ingredients.

Mustard Dressing

Serves 4
1 heaped tablespoon best Dijon or wholegrain mustard
2 tablespoons freshly squeezed lemon juice or balsamic vinegar
5 tablespoons olive oil
1 teaspoon salt
1 teaspoon freshly ground black pepper

Mix together all the ingredients.

Anchovy and Caper Dressing

Serves 4
2 tablespoons freshly squeezed lemon juice
5 tablespoons olive oil
1 teaspoon freshly ground black pepper
6 anchovy fillets, chopped or pounded
1 tablespoon small capers, chopped or pounded

Mix together all the ingredients in a bowl. Salt should not be needed because of the anchovies and capers.

Honey, Wholegrain Mustard and Garlic Dressing

Serves 4
½ teaspoon chopped or smashed garlic
1 tablespoon your favourite honey
1 tablespoon wholegrain mustard
2 tablespoons lemon juice
5 tablespoons olive oil

Mix together all the ingredients.

PASTA

My fascination with pasta began at Westminster College. There was a really cosmopolitan mix of students – almost half of them were on scholarships from overseas – which was interesting because everyone had a story to tell about the food they had grown up with. One of my best mates was Marco, who had Italian parents but had been brought up in London; he was a really good bloke and *so* passionate about Italy, the culture, the food and yes, you've guessed it, the *pasta*! I don't think he knew it, but he started my obsession. I began to read about pasta. I bought my first Italian pasta book. I was hooked. Everything about it was like an adventure; the shapes, sizes and colours were unlimited, and I was hungry to learn all about it. Since then I have continued to be excited by the versatility of pasta, but it's one of those things about which you'll never know it all; so I am always making it and picking up tips from different people.

As far as dried pasta goes, what can I say? Everyone has it in their cupboard – I know I do – and the Italians regard it very highly. Apart from being convenient, dried pasta has an excellent bite and is always good with fish and shellfish.

I really want you to make this pasta – it's very quick and simple and is something you're going to be really proud of. These are the two pastas I make at home. The ingredients are slightly different, but the method is the same and you can make them by hand, in your food processor or in your food mixer. Just remember, eggs and flour are always slightly different, so if you think it's a bit wet or sticky add a little more flour and if it's too dry add a little more egg. I always make far too much on purpose. I then dry it and keep it in airtight jars for really good, quick pasta.

Everyday Quick Pasta Recipe

Serves 4
500g/1lb strong pasta flour (Tipo '00')
5 fresh, large free-range eggs
semolina flour for dusting

Special Pasta Recipe

Serves 4
150g/5oz strong pasta flour (Tipo '00')
350g/12oz semolina flour (if you can't get hold of any
   semolina flour then plain flour will do)
2 large free-range eggs
9–10 large free-range egg yolks
semolina flour for dusting

Method (for both pasta recipes)

The making of pasta isn't some temperamental nightmare – you just chuck the eggs and flour together, no big deal. You don't need salt or oil, that's a factory fallacy. The only essential for the most superior pasta experience is the freshest free-range eggs and good, finely ground, strong flour and semolina flour. We will knead these ingredients to a smooth, fine and silky-textured dough, and work it enough to develop and strengthen the structure of the gluten in the dough to make it elastic.

If you are making pasta by hand, do it either on a clean surface or in a bowl. The whole process will take about 5 minutes. A processor or mixer will take even less time – quick, eh?

Making the dough

Stage 1 – By hand Make a well in the centre of the flour and add the eggs (and yolks if using the special recipe ingredients). Using a fork, break up the eggs slightly as you bring in the flour from the sides. As it begins to form a semi-soft dough, start to use your hands. Work the dough hard for about 3 minutes or until smooth, silky and elastic. Wrap it in clingfilm and allow it to rest in the fridge for 60 minutes.

Stage 1 – In a mixer Use the dough hook on the mixer. Add the flour to the eggs/yolks and mix at a medium speed for about 3 minutes or until it forms a tight dough. Take it out of the mixer and finish kneading by hand for about a minute or until smooth, silky and elastic. Wrap in clingfilm and allow to rest in the fridge for 60 minutes.

Stage 1 – In a food processor Plonk it all in and turn it on. Within 30 seconds, it should look like chewy-looking breadcrumbs. Leave it just a little longer to allow it to start working the gluten. It should now start to come together into larger balls of dough. Take it all out (the bowl should be clean) and work by hand for 2 minutes or until smooth, silky and elastic. Wrap in clingfilm and allow it to rest in the fridge for 60 minutes.

Stage 2 – With a rolling-pin Remove the dough from the fridge and divide into 2 balls. Re-cover one of the balls and, with the base of the palm of your hand, flatten the other one slightly. Lightly flour your clean surface and, with a rolling-pin, begin to roll out, always rolling away from you, dusting and turning 90°. Repeat this process until you have a very thin sheet of pasta – about 1–2mm thick, depending on what pasta variation you are making.

It does help to have a long, smooth and preferably heavy rolling-pin. When rolling the sheet of pasta out you can try to make it into a square shape but it's not that important. I actually think it is better to have the pasta looking handmade than looking perfect, like factory pasta.

Stage 2 – With a pasta machine Remove the dough from the fridge and divide into 4 balls. Re-cover 3 balls and work with one at a time. Flatten the ball slightly with the base of the palm of your hand and run the dough through the thickest setting on your pasta machine, which will roll it out into a thick sheet. What I do is fold the two ends into the middle and run the dough through, on the thickest setting, 3 or 4 times, which makes the sides of the pasta fill out to the full width of your pasta machine. Then I lightly dust both sides with flour and run it through the machine on a thinner setting. I repeat this through the settings until the sheets are 1–1.5mm thick. With a machine you can roll the sheets of pasta a lot thinner than you can by hand.

Persevere with the machine – it can be tricky, but it's worth it. They are really good value, last for ever and only cost around £25. Once you've cracked it you can easily knock up a bit of fresh pasta when you need it – it's quicker than walking down to the supermarket. It's just a question of understanding what the pasta does and how it reacts when you work with it.

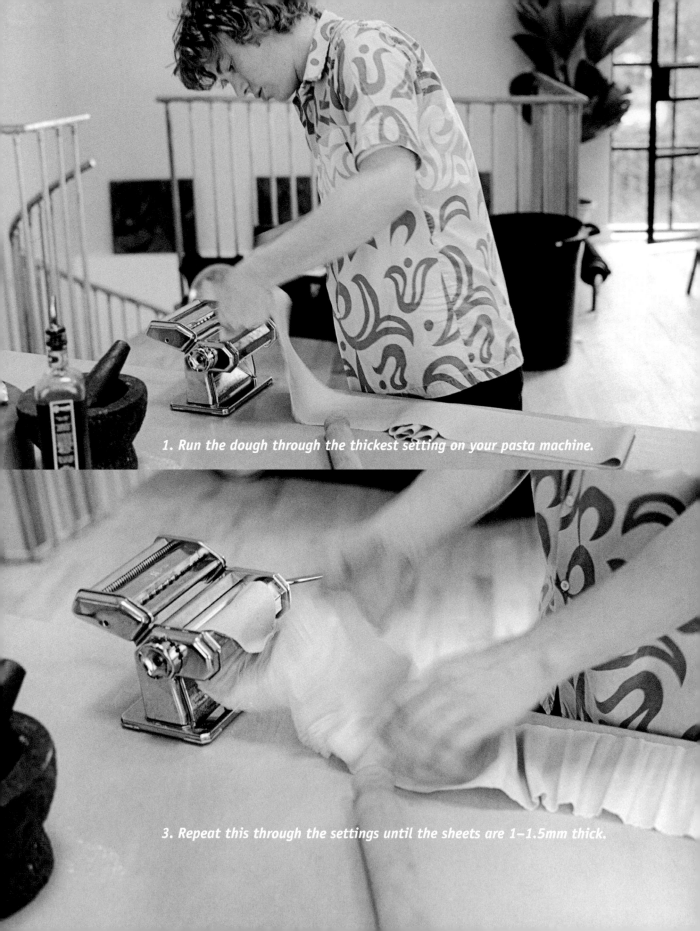

1. *Run the dough through the thickest setting on your pasta machine.*

3. *Repeat this through the settings until the sheets are 1–1.5mm thick.*

2. Fold the two ends into the middle and run the dough through.

4. With a machine you can roll the sheets
of pasta a lot thinner than you can by hand.

Herb Pasta

Add 4 good handfuls of fresh herbs finely chopped (one variety or any mixture). Proceed as in the basic recipe.

Beetroot Pasta

At last I've found something to do with those pre-cooked beetroot we sell so many of in Britain. Remove 2 of the eggs from the basic recipe and replace with roughly the equivalent amount of beetroot, peeled and puréed. Proceed as in the recipe, possibly having to adjust the flour to achieve a smooth, silky and elastic consistency.

Spinach Pasta

Remove 2 whole eggs from the basic recipe. Add approximately 300g/11oz spinach, which has been blanched, squeezed dry (a tea-towel is good for this) and finely chopped or puréed. Proceed as in the recipe, possibly having to adjust the flour to achieve a smooth, silky and elastic consistency.

Pepper Pasta

Add 1 level tablespoon of freshly ground black pepper. Proceed as in the basic recipe.

As far as I'm concerned these are all part of the same family and it is probably the most common pasta I make at home. Generally I tend to roll the pasta slightly thicker for pappardelle (about 1½mm thick), because I think it is a more robust pasta. I normally roll out tagliatelle and taglierini to about 1mm thick.

Having followed the basic recipe you should now have several sheets of pasta in front of you. Don't worry about trimming off any sides or corners, simply cut the sheets into approximately 20cm/8–9 inch lengths. Roll these up like swiss rolls, making sure you have dusted them generously both sides beforehand with semolina or flour.

If you are using a pasta machine you can run the sheets through its cutters. I prefer to cut it by hand so it's not all perfect and even.

Pappardelle

Cut each roll into slices approximately 4cm/1½ inches apart.

Tagliatelle

Cut each roll into slices approximately 2cm/¾ inch apart.

Taglierini

Cut each roll into slices approximately 1cm/⅜ inch apart.

When you've cut the pasta to your chosen width, gently toss and jiggle it about to separate the lengths of pasta and to remove any excess flour. Then place in portion-size heaps on a tray. The pasta can be cooked straight away or, if you place it on a tray and cover it with a very well-wrung-out damp cloth, it will stay fresh for about 3–4 hours. Alternatively it can be dried (thoroughly) for 3–4 hours and stored in an airtight container, where it will keep for at least 2 months.

Pappardelle with Dried Porcini and Thyme, Tomato and Mascarpone Sauce

The simple addition of dried porcini and thyme can turn plain tomato sauce into something much more interesting.

Serves 4
55g/2oz dried porcini
1 tablespoon olive oil
1 clove of garlic, finely chopped
1 good handful of thyme, picked
¾ tomato sauce recipe (see page 237)
2 tablespoons mascarpone
salt and freshly ground black pepper
455g/1lb pappardelle (see basic pasta recipes, page 47)
fresh Parmesan cheese, grated

Dried porcini are available in nearly all supermarkets and good delis. Look for good-looking, well-shaped mushrooms – avoid packs with broken-up pieces, containing bits of dirt. Place the dried mushrooms in a small bowl and add about 285ml/½ pint boiling water. Make sure all the mushrooms are submerged, and leave them for 10–15 minutes.

Put the olive oil and garlic into a thick-bottomed, semi-hot pan and allow to cook without colouring. Pick out the soaked porcini (reserving the liquor), shake off any excess moisture and add to the pan with the thyme – be careful because it will spit a little. Stir and fry. As the garlic begins to colour, gently pour in some of the liquor that you soaked your mushrooms in (don't use the dregs as they may contain some dirt, just gently pour off the first three-quarters into your pan and discard the rest). Allow the mushrooms to cook down gently to nearly nothing and then add the tomato sauce (this is a great sauce, quite substantial and smoky in flavour). Add the mascarpone and taste for seasoning.

Meanwhile cook the pappardelle in boiling salted water until al dente. Add to the sauce and toss. Serve immediately, sprinkled with Parmesan.

Pappardelle with Mixed Wild Mushrooms

These days there seems to be more and more of a choice of wild mushrooms in the supermarkets. They are not always stored and displayed as I think they should be – I don't like sweaty mushrooms in plastic containers – but I'm sure things will get better. Even as a chef I am surprised to see pieds de moutons, girolles and trompettes des morts popping up throughout the year as well as the more predictable blewits, shitake, chestnut, field and oyster mushrooms – there is a lot of choice. If you are a vegetarian, mushrooms can be a very interesting, fulfilling, gutsy and even *meaty* part of your diet.

Serves 4
250–300g/9–11oz mushrooms (I would probably buy around 400g/14oz of
    mushrooms, as you have to trim a bit off)
3 tablespoons olive oil
1 clove of garlic, finely chopped
1–2 small dried red chillies, pounded or very finely chopped
salt and freshly ground black pepper
juice of ½ lemon
455g/1lb pappardelle (see basic pasta recipes, page 47)
a small handful of grated Parmesan cheese
1 handful of fresh parsley, roughly chopped
55g/2oz unsalted butter

Brush off any dirt from the mushrooms with a pastry brush or a tea-towel. Slice the mushrooms thinly, but tear girolles, chanterelles and blewits in half. Put the olive oil in a very hot frying pan and add the mushrooms. Let them fry fast, tossing once or twice, then add the garlic and chilli with a pinch of salt (it is very important to season mushrooms *slightly*, as it really brings out the flavour). Continue to fry fast for 4–5 minutes, tossing regularly. Then turn the heat off and squeeze in the lemon juice. Toss and season to taste.

Meanwhile cook the pasta in boiling, salted water until al dente. Add to the mushrooms, with the Parmesan, parsley and butter. Toss gently, coating the pasta with the mushrooms and their flavour. Serve, scraping out all of the last bits of mushroom from the pan, and sprinkle with a little extra parsley and Parmesan.

Pappardelle with Sweet Leeks and Mascarpone

When buying leeks try to buy the medium/smaller ones which are sweeter, more tender and basically nicer to eat.

Serves 4
1 small knob of butter
1 tablespoon olive oil
4 medium leeks, trimmed, washed and sliced at an angle
1 clove of garlic, finely chopped
salt and freshly ground black pepper
200g/7oz mascarpone
455g/1lb pappardelle (see basic pasta recipes, page 47)
1 handful of Parmesan cheese

Put the butter and olive oil into a semi-hot, thick-bottomed pan, add the leeks and garlic, with a pinch of salt, and gently sweat, without colouring, for about 5–10 minutes with a lid on, until the leeks are soft and sweet. Add the mascarpone. Let this gently melt into the leeks, creating a semi-thick sauce. Taste for seasoning.

Meanwhile cook the pasta in boiling, salted water until al dente. Toss gently in the sauce (if it seems slightly thick, add a little of the cooking water from the pasta). The sauce should perfectly coat the pappardelle. Serve sprinkled generously with Parmesan.

Tagliatelle with Baby Courgettes, Lemon and Basil

This is a light, fragrant and very quickly made pasta dish using very firm baby courgettes, which hardly need to be cooked at all. The idea is to slice them as thinly as possible in an irregular fashion. The big fat courgettes, which are fluffy inside, won't do at all for this recipe.

Serves 4
4 tablespoons olive oil
1 clove of garlic, finely chopped
8–10 small, very firm courgettes
juice of 1 lemon
1 good handful of fresh basil, picked
455g/1lb tagliatelle (see basic pasta recipes, page 47)
salt and freshly ground black pepper
90g/3½oz Parmesan cheese, grated

Put the olive oil and garlic into a semi-hot, thick-bottomed pan and fry for about 30 seconds without colouring, then add your baby courgettes and toss gently. After about 2 minutes squeeze in the juice of the lemon, add the basil, and cook a little longer.

Meanwhile cook the tagliatelle in salted boiling water until al dente. Toss it with the courgettes to mix the flavours, season to taste and add the Parmesan to round all the flavours together – you may need a little extra olive oil to loosen it. Serve with some torn basil and a sprinkling of Parmesan on top.

Beetroot Tagliatelle with Pesto, Mussels and White Wine

I learnt this recipe from an Italian friend of mine who lives in Florence. The colours are quite interesting and the mussels and pesto work surprisingly well together, so it is definitely worth trying – and it is very quick to make.

Serves 4
3 tablespoons olive oil
455g/1lb fresh, live mussels (washed, cleaned and debearded)
1 clove of garlic, finely sliced
150ml/5–6fl oz dry white wine
1 small knob of butter
2 good handfuls of flat-leaf parsley, roughly chopped
455g/1lb beetroot tagliatelle (see basic pasta recipes and variations,
*   pages 47 and 53)*
salt and freshly ground black pepper
pesto (see page 232)

Put the olive oil into a very hot, thick-bottomed, high-sided pan, and straight away add the mussels and garlic. Place a lid on and shake for around 20 seconds – it will sizzle furiously. Then add the white wine. Replace the lid, and leave on the fast heat for about 1–2 minutes. This will steam open the mussels (discard any unopened ones). Add the knob of butter and the parsley and remove from the heat.

Meanwhile cook the beetroot tagliatelle in boiling, salted water until al dente. Gently toss the tagliatelle and mussels together until the juices just coat the pasta, then check for seasoning and serve with a generous spoonful of pesto on top.

Tagliatelle with Peas, Broad Beans, Cream and Parmesan

Serves 4
150g/5–6oz fresh peas
150g/5–6oz broad beans, as fresh as you can get
2 tablespoons olive oil
1 clove of garlic
200ml/7fl oz double cream
1 small handful of mint
150g/5–6oz Parmesan cheese
salt and freshly ground black pepper
455g/1lb tagliatelle (see basic pasta recipes, page 47)

First of all pod your peas and broad beans. If the peas are small baby ones don't bother blanching them, but if they're slightly tough, blanch them in unsalted boiling water until tender. Do the same with the broad beans, and if you think the skins on the larger beans are tough, remove them after blanching. Take half the peas and broad beans and smash, chop or whizz in a food processor until semi-smooth.

Put the olive oil and garlic into a thick-bottomed, semi-hot pan. Cook for a few moments without colouring, then add the smashed up peas and broad beans. Toss them around for 1 minute then add the double cream and the remainder of the peas and broad beans. Stir in the mint and allow to simmer. Add half the Parmesan and taste for seasoning.

Meanwhile cook the tagliatelle in boiling, salted water until al dente and add to the sauce – it should just coat the pasta. Serve with a little extra Parmesan sprinkled on top.

Buttered Taglierini with Seared Scallops, White Wine, Chilli and Parsley

This dish takes only minutes to cook. Get everything ready and then begin. Make sure you don't overcook the scallops.

Serves 4
12 scallops, trimmed with roe on or off to your preference
1 tablespoon olive oil
1 clove of garlic, peeled and finely chopped
2 medium/large fresh red chillies, deseeded and finely chopped
2 good glasses of white wine
455g/1lb taglierini (see basic pasta recipes, page 47)
1 good handful of flat-leaf parsley, roughly chopped
55–85g/2–3oz butter
salt and freshly ground black pepper

On a board, place each scallop on its flat side and slice it across in half. Put the olive oil into a hot pan and add the scallops, garlic and chilli, which will sear and sizzle straight away. As soon as the scallops have coloured on one side pour in the wine, letting it reduce slightly.

Meanwhile cook the taglierini in boiling, salted water until al dente. Add the pasta to the scallops with the parsley and butter and remove from the heat. Toss and taste for seasoning. Serve.

Taglierini with Pan-cooked Red Mullet, Sun-dried Tomatoes, Chilli, Parsley and Black Olives

Serves 4

6 tablespoons olive oil
4 fillets of red mullet, roughly 170–225g/6–8oz each, scaled, filleted and pinboned
2 medium/large fresh red chillies, deseeded and finely sliced
1 clove of garlic, finely sliced
1 handful of sun-dried tomatoes, roughly sliced
1 good handful of your favourite black olives
1 glass of white wine
455g/1lb taglierini (see basic pasta recipes, page 47)
salt and freshly ground black pepper
1 good handful of flat-leaf parsley, very finely chopped
a little extra virgin olive oil

Put the olive oil into a moderately hot thick-bottomed pan and add the red mullet, skin side up. Sprinkle in the chilli, garlic, sun-dried tomatoes and olives. Allow to fry gently for about 2 minutes, without letting the garlic colour. Then add the white wine, put a lid on the pan and allow to simmer for a further 3 minutes.

Meanwhile cook the taglierini in boiling salted water until al dente. Push the red mullet to one side, tilt the pan slightly so that all the lovely juices and cooking liquor gather at the opposite side, and toss in the taglierini. Once it is nicely coated, taste for seasoning and add most of the parsley. Gently fold in the red mullet. Serve sprinkled with the rest of the chopped parsley on top, and a drizzle of extra virgin olive oil.

In Britain ravioli has been, and often still is, thought of as just pasta filled with minced meat and covered with tomato sauce – a baked bean substitute, a quick snack between meals, something to warm up when you can't be bothered to cook anything else. But ravioli is much more than that. They are sexy little special things, they're like little presents, but they have to be nice presents if you know what I mean. What I'm trying to say is that, after going to the trouble of making your own lovely pasta, you should fill it with a classy and fresh filling. Ravioli is very diverse, so the flavours can be strong, light or fragrant; just be tasteful in your choice, using the best seasonal ingredients. In Italy ravioli is a delicacy: regions, towns, villages and restaurants can be famous for particular shapes and sizes.

The most important thing about ravioli is it *must* be sealed completely. If the edges aren't sealed or cracks appear in the pasta (which can sometimes happen, as different textures of filling can be harder to cover and seal), boiling water will leak in and ruin your tasty filling.

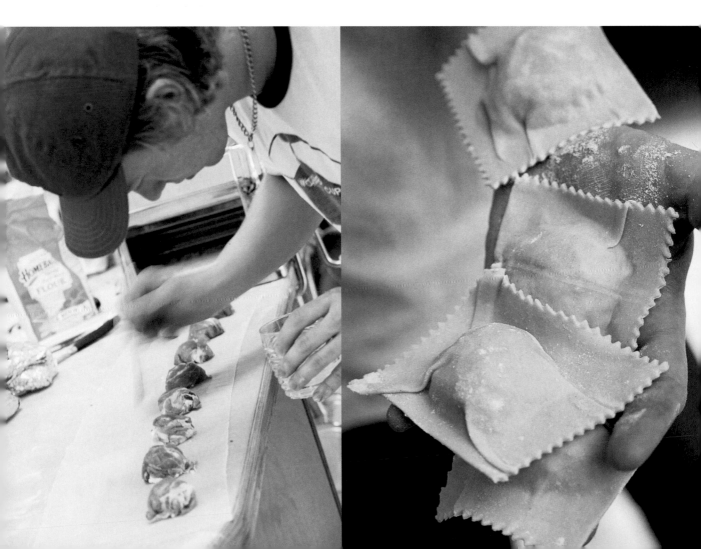

Roll out several sheets of pasta, about 1mm thick, and make small batches of 4–5 ravioli at a time, covering the extra sheets with a damp cloth. I normally make them around 7 × 7cm/3 × 3 inches – your sheets of pasta if made in a machine will generally be about 10cm/4 inches wide, which gives you a little extra to mould around your filling and trim. Lay out your pasta on a generously dusted surface and place a good heaped teaspoon of filling in the middle of the sheet at one end. Repeat this all the way along the pasta, spacing 5cm/2 inches apart. Then, using a clean pastry brush and some water (not egg, I don't know who invented that, it's a horrible idea), *lightly* but evenly brush the pasta. (It's the water which will stick your pasta together, and common sense should tell you that if this isn't done correctly you won't be able to seal it properly.) Lay another similar-sized sheet of pasta on top of the first.

At this point you should try to have a gentle touch (watch out for long nails and rings). With your thumb or the base of your palm, gently pat the pasta down on the long side farthest away from you. Starting from one side, with the small-finger side of your hand, push the pasta down at one end, then slowly curl your fingers and your palm surrounding the filling, eventually cupping and gently pushing down on the other side of the filling. (This sounds like a palaver but it is not, it takes seconds and is an extremely effective way of extracting all the air and ensuring that the ravioli is tightly sealed.) Repeat along the length of the pasta, making sure it hasn't stuck to the work-surface. Then trim and cut the ravioli into shape with a knife or crinkly cutter.

Now you've made your ravioli you can cook it straight away, generally for about 3–4 minutes in salted, *gently* boiling water. Or you can store it uncooked in the fridge for 3–4 hours on a tray generously dusted with semolina, if you want to eat it later.

Ravioli with Prosciutto, Sun-dried Tomatoes, Basil and Mozzarella

I am afraid that this is a clichéd and obvious combination but it is quick and bloody good, so try it. The secret, as usual, is in using the best ingredients, especially the freshest mozzarella.

Serves 4
1 handful of Parmesan cheese, finely grated
1 good handful of fresh basil, picked and torn
12 sun-dried tomatoes, roughly chopped
2 balls (200g/7oz) buffalo mozzarella, roughly chopped
salt and freshly ground black pepper
10 good slices of prosciutto, fat removed
455g/1lb basic pasta recipe (see page 47)
olive oil
extra basil and Parmesan cheese to serve

Put the Parmesan, basil, sun-dried tomatoes and mozzarella in a bowl, stir together and season to taste. Cut the slices of prosciutto in half. Place 1 heaped teaspoon of the filling mix at one end of a piece of prosciutto, then fold in the sides and roll up so that the filling is enclosed. Repeat with the rest of the filling and prosciutto – you should have about 20 small balls. Fill the ravioli (see opposite page) and cook in gently boiling salted water for about 3–4 minutes, until tender. Drain carefully.

   Serve sprinkled with olive oil, black pepper, freshly shaved Parmesan, and torn basil.

Ravioli of Borage, Stinging Nettles, Marjoram and Fresh Ricotta

This is delicious and you should try it. When young borage and stinging nettle leaves are picked (with a pair of Marigolds – mmm, very nice), washed and plunged into boiling salted water, they lose all their sting – they feel like spinach but hold most of their shape and texture. Chopped and slowly fried with a little butter, marjoram and garlic stinging nettles are absolutely excellent.

Serves 4–6
2 good handfuls of young stinging nettle leaves
2 good handfuls of young borage leaves
2 tablespoons olive oil
1 knob of butter
1 clove of garlic, chopped
1 handful of fresh marjoram, picked
salt and freshly ground black pepper
freshly grated nutmeg to taste
400g/14oz ricotta cheese
100g/3–4oz Parmesan cheese
455g/1lb basic pasta recipe (see page 47)
extra butter and Parmesan to serve

After carefully picking your stinging nettles and borage leaves, wash them well in water and then plunge them into boiling salted water for 30 seconds. This will wilt the leaves and will take away the sting (don't be tempted to cook them for too long). Drain them in a colander and remove any excess water by squeezing them in a tea-towel. Roughly chop and put into a semi-warm, thick-bottomed pan with the olive oil, butter, garlic and marjoram. Cook gently, seasoning as you go, and adding the nutmeg to taste. After a couple of minutes it should be tasting very flavoursome. Remove from the heat and allow to cool.

   Once the nettles and borage have cooled, fork in your ricotta, add the final seasoning and Parmesan to taste and toss gently. Fill the ravioli (see page 65) and cook in boiling salted water for 3–4 minutes, until tender. Serve 3 or 4 ravioli per person, with some knobs of butter over the top and some grated Parmesan. I like to pick the purple borage flowers, fry them until crisp in clarified butter (see page 227), and scatter them over the pasta before serving.

Ravioli of Smashed Broad Beans, Mint and Ricotta

Serves 6
255g/9oz podded broad beans, plus extra for garnish
1 small handful of mint, picked and chopped
1 tablespoon olive oil
150g/5–6oz ricotta cheese
1 handful of grated Parmesan cheese, or to taste
juice of 1 lemon
salt and freshly ground black pepper
455g/1lb basic pasta recipe (see page 47)
extra chopped mint, olive oil and Parmesan cheese to serve

If the broad beans are very small and soft, you can use them raw. If they are medium to large, blanch them until just tender in unsalted boiling water (remove the skins after blanching if they are slightly tough). Smash or finely chop half the beans and leave the other half whole.

Put all the beans into a bowl with the chopped mint (added to taste), olive oil and ricotta. Lightly fork this through, adding the Parmesan, lemon juice and seasoning to taste. Stuff the ravioli with the filling (see page 65) and cook them in gently boiling salted water for around 3–4 minutes, until tender. Drain carefully.

Serve drizzled with a little extra olive oil, and scattered with the extra broad beans, some chopped mint and some freshly grated or shaved Parmesan.

Ravioli with Potato, Watercress and Cheeses

Make a point of using two delicious, contrasting cheeses, for example a strong cheese like Gorgonzola or a creamy taleggio and a hard cheese such as pecorino or Parmesan.

Serves 4–6
570g/1¼lb boiling potatoes (Maris Piper, Desirée)
4 cloves of garlic, peeled
salt and freshly ground black pepper
55g/2oz butter
150g/5–6oz cheese (two varieties, see above)
grated nutmeg to taste
2 or 3 good handfuls of watercress, large stalks removed
455g/1lb basic pasta recipe (see page 47)
extra olive oil or butter, cheese and watercress to serve

Wash and peel the potatoes, put them into very salted, boiling water with the garlic and cook until the potatoes are just tender (it is very important not to under- or overcook them). Drain them for about 5 minutes to enable the excess water to evaporate (if you overcook them or don't drain them correctly they'll be too moist and your filling will be too wet).

When the potatoes have cooled slightly add your butter and your chosen cheeses. Stir and fork through to mix and break the potatoes up (I like to leave the mixture slightly chunky). Add the nutmeg and seasoning to taste. Stir in the watercress, half finely chopped and the rest coarsely chopped. Stuff the ravioli with a good heaped teaspoon of this mixture and cook in boiling salted water for about 3–4 minutes, until tender.

Serve with some extra olive oil or butter, some more of your chosen cheese grated over the top and some ripped up watercress.

Tortellini are quite similar to ravioli; however, once made, they seem to hold themselves together slightly better. This means, for example, that they can be tossed in herbed butters or added to salads – they are a lot more resilient than ravioli and can be incorporated into a wider range of dishes.

Making tortellini

Roll out several sheets of pasta about 1mm thick. With a sharp knife cut your pasta sheets into equal sized squares or circles (about 10cm/4 inches in diameter, or whatever size you want). You can do this with all your sheets of pasta and make them all at the same time, or do them in batches, keeping the other sheets under a damp cloth. Place a good teaspoon of filling just off-centre. With a clean pastry brush and some water, lightly and evenly brush around the edges of your pasta. You must do this thoroughly otherwise the pasta will not seal. Fold the shape in half, enclosing the filling, and if they look a bit uneven don't worry (I think that is nice because they look home-made not factory-made). To extract the air and make sure that the tortellini are tightly sealed, cup your hand around the mound of filling and slowly curl in your fingers, squeezing all the air out. Gently press down the open end to finish sealing the pasta (if there are any cracks or tears in the pasta it will burst open during cooking, so just remove the filling and start again). Fold in the two 'flaps' and squeeze together. You have your tortellini. These can now be cooked straight away, generally for about 3–4 minutes in salted, slowly boiling water, or you can store them on a semolina-dusted tray in the fridge for about 3–4 hours if you want to cook them later.

Mixed Cheese and Basil Tortellini with a Fresh and Chunky Tomato Sauce

Some of the worst tortellini that I have tried have been mixed cheese ones. I must admit they've always been from supermarkets or horrible delis, and they've been filled with leftover or really rubbery cheap cheese. This tortellini recipe is absolutely superb, because you choose and balance the cheeses to your own taste. Choose different mixtures – strong cheeses, creamy cheeses – a combination that you enjoy eating. Remember, when cheese cooks it melts and some cheeses, such as fontina, have better melting qualities. The fresh tomato sauce is great because, as well as giving a lot of flavour, it also cuts through the fattiness of the cheese.

Serves 4–6
55g/2oz fontina cheese
55g/2oz pecorino cheese
55g/2oz Parmesan cheese
55g/2oz ricotta cheese
2 good handfuls of fresh basil, picked
salt and freshly ground black pepper
455g/1lb basic pasta recipe (see page 47)
1 tomato sauce recipe (see page 237)
extra olive oil and Parmesan cheese to serve

Grate or finely chop (if necessary) the cheeses and add to a bowl with three-quarters of the basil, torn up. It is always a good idea to add one binding cheese such as ricotta to your mixture, as this helps to hold it all together. Season with a little pepper. Then fill your tortellini (see page 72) and cook in boiling salted water for 3–4 minutes, until tender. You should be able to cook your tomato sauce, once prepared, in the same amount of time that it takes to cook the tortellini. When the tortellini are cooked, drain them, add the tomato sauce, and toss. Add the remaining fresh basil (whole) and toss again.

Serve with a little extra olive oil and some Parmesan cheese.

Spicy Squash, Basil and Ricotta Tortellini with Crispy Herbs

Serves 4–6
1 spicy roasted squash recipe (see page 148)
2 good handfuls of fresh basil, picked and roughly chopped
255g/9oz ricotta cheese (the best you can find)
1–2 handfuls of grated Parmesan cheese, to taste
salt and freshly ground black pepper
455g/1lb basic pasta recipe (see page 47)
2 handfuls of mixed fresh herbs (sage, thyme, marjoram)

Divide the spicy roasted squash in half and finely chop one half, leaving the other coarsely chopped (you can remove the skin if you wish but I love it because it goes soft and chewy). Put all the squash into a bowl with the basil, ricotta and most of the Parmesan. Fork through and taste for seasoning. Fill your tortellini (see page 72) and cook in boiling salted water for 3–4 minutes, until tender.

Fry off the mixed herbs in a little butter, clarified butter (see page 227) or olive oil until crispy and scatter over your tortellini. You can serve with a little extra Parmesan on top.

Minted Creamed Asparagus and Ricotta Tortellini with Asparagus Tips and Butter

This is an excellent dish. The sad thing about asparagus is that they are always very highly trimmed and you lose a lot of stalk, but this dish uses asparagus to its full.

Serves 4–6
2 really good bunches of asparagus (weighing around 700g/1½lb)
olive oil
85g/3oz butter
1 clove of garlic, finely chopped
salt and freshly ground black pepper
400g/14oz ricotta cheese
1½ good handfuls of fresh mint, finely chopped
100g/3–4oz Parmesan cheese
455g/1lb basic pasta recipe (see page 47)
extra Parmesan cheese to serve

First of all wash the asparagus; it is surprising how many little bits of grit can be on the buds, so wash the buds and give the stalks a quick wash too. Then, gathering your asparagus up, cut off the tips about 6cm/2½ to 3 inches from the top and put to one side. Carefully peel away any stringy bits from the stalks and discard. Finely slice the stalks across and sauté gently with a little olive oil, some of the butter and all the garlic. Once the asparagus stalks are well cooked, even semi-mushy, add a little seasoning and allow to cool.

Once cooled, place the stalks in a bowl with the ricotta, three-quarters of the mint and the Parmesan. Fold everything together and check for seasoning. Fill the tortellini (see page 72) and cook in boiling, salted water for about 3–4 minutes, until tender. While the tortellini are cooking, place the asparagus tips into boiling water and cook until tender. Toss the tips into a bowl with a little salt and the remaining butter, and spoon over your tortellini.

Lovely with a little extra Parmesan grated over the top and the remaining chopped mint if you like.

Spinach Tortellini with Ricotta, Summer Herbs and Parmesan

Serves 4–6
400g/14oz fresh ricotta cheese (the best you can find)
¼ clove of garlic
½ dried red chilli
salt and freshly ground black pepper
4 large handfuls of fresh basil, picked and finely chopped
2 handfuls of fresh marjoram or oregano, picked and roughly chopped
2 handfuls of fresh flat-leaf parsley, picked and roughly chopped
1 handful of fresh mint, picked and roughly chopped
1–2 good handfuls of freshly grated Parmesan cheese, to taste
455g/1lb spinach pasta (see basic pasta recipes and variations, pages 47 and 53)
butter to serve

Put the ricotta, garlic, chilli, salt, pepper, most of the herbs and three-quarters of the Parmesan into a bowl and lightly fork through. Adjust the salt, pepper, Parmesan and chilli to get a good balance. This should be a very light filling but full of flavour. You can increase the flavour by pounding a quarter of the fresh herbs in a pestle and mortar. The pounded herbs will also add a little colour to your mixture, which is quite nice. Fill your tortellini (see page 72) and cook in boiling salted water for 3–4 minutes, until tender. When they are cooked, serve them in a bowl, sprinkled with the remaining herbs, small knobs of butter and the rest of the Parmesan.

FARFALLE

I like to roll out the pasta for farfalle to about 1½mm thick. Making the characteristic farfalle shape is very, very simple – it can be done with a knife or you can use one of those rolly, jagged cutters.

Making farfalle

Trim all 4 sides of the sheet of pasta with a knife, just to tidy it up a bit, then lay out the sheet lengthwise in front of you. Decide what size you want to make the farfalle – do you want small ones for soups or do you want medium or large ones? It really doesn't matter, it's up to you, this is why home-made pasta is so nice because you can choose. I normally cut down the length of the sheet of pasta to make 3 strips about 4cm/1½ inches wide. Leaving the 3 sheets of pasta together, cut across at right angles to the first cuts, about 7½cm/3 inches apart, all the way down, using a knife or a pasta cutter.

What you will now have in front of you is lots of little rectangular sheets of pasta all next to each other. To make the characteristic farfalle bow-tie shape, carefully pinch together each side of the pasta in the middle making sure that it holds its shape – this can be done very fast.

Allow the farfalle to dry slightly for about 5 minutes and they will be fresh, soft and ready to cook straight away. Alternatively you can place them on a tray lightly dusted with semolina, and put a damp cloth on top – they will then stay fresh for about 3–4 hours if you want to cook them later. Or just place them on a rack or tray, allow them to dry thoroughly for about 2–3 hours, and store them in an airtight container. Properly dried, farfalle will keep for at least 2 months.

Farfalle with a Quick Tomato Sauce

This tomato sauce is made from fresh, perfectly ripe tomatoes. It's not as rich in flavour as the tomato sauce recipe on page 237, as it is made so quickly, which makes it a lot lighter, more delicate and fragrant in taste. It can be cooked down so that it is semi-chunky, or can be quickly whizzed up in a food processor for a smooth sauce.

Serves 4–6
4 tablespoons extra virgin olive oil
6–8 medium/large tomatoes
1 clove of garlic, finely chopped
salt and freshly ground black pepper
2 good handfuls of fresh basil, picked and torn
455g/1lb farfalle (see basic pasta recipes, page 47)
extra virgin olive oil to serve
a little grated Parmesan cheese

Put the olive oil into a hot, thick-bottomed pan. While the oil is heating up, wash the tomatoes, remove the cores and roughly chop. Add the garlic to the pan, let it soften, and before it starts to colour add your tomatoes. They will sizzle and spit and begin to cook down. Bring to the boil and cook quickly for around 5 minutes. You can leave the sauce chunky or you can semi-purée or completely purée it in a food processor or mixer. While the sauce is still hot, check for seasoning and add most of the basil.

Meanwhile cook the farfalle in boiling salted water until al dente and drain. Add to the tomato sauce, toss, and serve sprinkled with the reserved basil, a little extra virgin olive oil, freshly ground black pepper and a little grated Parmesan.

Farfalle with Artichokes, Parmesan, Garlic and Cream

Serves 4
4 medium/large globe artichokes, thinly sliced
2 tablespoons olive oil
1 large clove of garlic, finely chopped
1 tablespoon chopped fresh thyme
small squeeze of lemon juice
200ml/7fl oz double cream
½ tablespoon chopped fresh mint
150g/5–6oz Parmesan cheese, grated
salt and freshly ground black pepper
455g/1lb farfalle (see basic pasta recipes, page 47 and farfalle, page 78)

Prepare the artichokes (see page 137). Slice in half, then finely slice from the core to the top. Heat the olive oil in a thick-bottomed pan and add the garlic and thyme. Add the artichokes, and cook gently, without colouring, until tender. Add the lemon juice and cook for 1 minute. Add the cream and most of the mint and simmer for a minute, then remove from the heat and add half the Parmesan. Season to taste with a little salt and some freshly ground black pepper.

Meanwhile cook the farfalle in boiling salted water for 3–4 minutes or until al dente. Toss in the sauce and serve sprinkled with the remaining mint and the rest of the Parmesan.

Farfalle with Watercress and Rocket Pesto

Serves 4
455g/1lb farfalle (see basic pasta recipes, page 47)
grated Parmesan to serve

Watercress and Rocket Pesto
¼ clove of garlic, chopped
1 handful of fresh basil, picked
1 handful of rocket
1 handful of watercress, picked
1 handful of roasted pine nuts
1 good handful of grated Parmesan cheese
extra virgin olive oil
small squeeze of lemon juice
salt and freshly ground black pepper

First make the pesto. Pound the garlic in a pestle and mortar with the basil, rocket and watercress. Add the roasted pine nuts and pound again. Turn out into a bowl and add half the Parmesan. Stir this in and add enough olive oil to bind the sauce. Taste, and add a little salt and pepper and the remaining Parmesan. Add the lemon juice if it needs it.

Cook the farfalle in boiling salted water for 3–4 minutes or until al dente. Toss the pasta in the pesto, and serve sprinkled with Parmesan.

FISH AND
SHELLFISH

Skate Wings with Prosciutto, Radicchio, Capers and Lemon

Make sure the skate is really fresh and cook it the day you buy it. Choose skate wings weighing about 340g/12oz, as there's quite a lot of bone in the middle; ask your fishmonger to take off the middle knuckles and trim the wings.

Serves 4
4 × 340g/12oz wings of skate
salt and freshly ground black pepper
a little flour for dusting
4 tablespoons olive oil
5 knobs of butter
9–12 slices of prosciutto or parma ham
1 clove of garlic, finely chopped
1 head of radicchio
2 tablespoons capers, soaked in water
juice of 2 lemons

Rinse the skate wings, pat dry and season with salt and pepper. Lightly dust with flour, shaking off any excess. Get the pan really hot, add the oil, then add four knobs of butter and the skate together and turn down the heat to medium high. Cook for about 2 minutes on each side, until the skate is nicely coloured. (If all the wings don't fit in your pan together, you will need to repeat this process, using 1 tablespoon of oil and 1 knob of butter as you cook each wing and giving the pan a quick wipe in between with some kitchen paper.) Place all the skate on a roasting tray and then finish off in the oven, at 230°C/450°F/gas 8, for about 4–5 minutes or until the flesh just pulls away from the bone.

   Slice the prosciutto and radicchio finely. Using the pan again, fry the prosciutto until golden, then add the garlic, radicchio and capers; reduce the heat and add the last knob of butter. The prosciutto should slightly crispen and the radicchio will wilt. Add the lemon juice and immediately tip over the skate wings. Lovely!

Pan-seared Scallops with Crispy Bacon and Sage, Puy Lentils and Green Salad

Every now and again at the River Café we make this dish, and I think it's the best scallop dish in the whole world – I've never ever tasted anything better. Here's my version. The combination is superb, it's not heavy and it's full of different flavours. I think pan-fried or pan-seared is the only way to eat scallops because the skin goes really caramelly and sweet. You must try this, even though scallops are quite expensive – everything else in the recipe is really cheap and you only need 2 or 3 scallops per person. It is a really interesting and quick thing to make.

Serves 4
12 thin slices of streaky bacon or pancetta
2 tablespoons olive oil
8 leaves of fresh sage per person
12 scallops
salt and freshly ground black pepper
juice of 1 lemon
8 heaped tablespoons cooked lentils (see page 162)
4 large handfuls of green salad leaves
olive oil and lemon juice dressing (see page 42)

Fry the bacon or pancetta in a small amount of olive oil in a hot pan. When it's nearly ready, add the sage. The bacon and sage will cook and crisp up at about the same time. Once they are cooked, take them out of the pan and put them on to kitchen paper to drain.

Put the pan back on the heat and, when it is very hot, add a little drizzle of oil and fry the seasoned scallops. These will take about a minute each side; the skin will go slightly crisp and golden brown. When you've cooked both sides of your scallops, squeeze the lemon juice over the top and give them a stir – this will start to caramelize the outside skin even more. Take the scallops out of the pan and put them into a dish.

Using the same pan, re-heat the lentils. Dress the salad leaves with the olive oil and lemon dressing and divide between 4 plates. Sprinkle the crispy bacon and the crispy sage leaves over the 4 salad plates and then put the scallops round the salad. When your lentils are hot, just sprinkle on top. This should be eaten straight away.

Fast-roasted Cod with Parsley, Oregano, Chilli and Lime

This is a very quick and simple way to cook cod. The trick is to get a really nice thick steak of cod, as fresh as possible – I look for steaks about 3cm/1¼ inches thick.

Serves 4
4 cod steaks, 255–340g/9–12oz each in weight
1–2 tablespoons olive oil
½ tablespoon dried oregano
2 good handfuls of fresh flat-leaf parsley, very finely chopped
1 medium/large fresh red chilli, deseeded and finely chopped
salt and freshly ground black pepper
2 limes

Wash the cod steaks in a little cold water and pat dry with kitchen paper. Using your hand, rub the olive oil into the cod steaks so that they are very lightly coated. Put the oregano, parsley and chilli into a bowl and mix. Season the cod steaks and pat with the herb mixture.

Preheat the oven and a roasting tray to 225°C/425°F/gas 7. Put the cod steaks into the roasting tray – they will sear and sizzle immediately. Add the halved limes to the tray and replace in the oven on a top shelf, to slightly colour the top of the fish. Cook for 10 minutes. When cooked, serve with the roasted limes, which you can squeeze over the fish before serving.

This cod is really nice with some plainly boiled potatoes, simply cooked greens or a salad and some homemade aïoli (see page 229).

Pan-fried Fillet of Cod with Parsley, Capers and Brown Butter

This is a very fast, simple and classic dish – you can't really go wrong with it.

Serves 4
4 × 225g/8oz fillet steaks of cod, skinned and pinboned
salt and freshly ground black pepper
flour
2 tablespoons olive oil
85g/3oz butter
1 good handful of capers, soaked in water
1 good handful of fresh flat-leaf parsley, picked
2 lemons

For this recipe it is important to have a trusty frying-pan that you can heat until very hot. Season the cod fillets on both sides and very lightly dust with flour, shaking off the excess. Add the olive oil to the hot pan, swirling it around so that the bottom is completely coated. Place the cod in the pan, flesh side down, and leave for 2 minutes, just checking the underside with a fork to make sure it is colouring nicely. When the first side is nice and golden, turn the fish on to the skin side and carry on cooking, turning the heat down slightly. After about 3–4 minutes the cod should be just cooked. Remove the cod from the pan and keep it warm.

Toss in the butter and allow this to melt into the pan and begin to colour slightly. Add the capers and parsley and, for the next 30 seconds, just swirl the pan around until the butter begins to go slightly brown (not black). Squeeze in the juice of 1 lemon and remove from the heat; it will sizzle and bubble. Swirl the juices around in the pan then pour the capers, parsley and brown butter over the cod. Serve with lemon quarters, boiled potatoes and a big green salad.

Roasted Trout with Thyme

I think trout's a really enjoyable thing to eat, especially when you have it whole. I remember going fishing with my grandad when I was about seven years old – we used to catch trout, take it home and cook it immediately. There is nothing like a plainly cooked piece of trout, but trout with thyme is a really subtle and refreshing combination. The last time I cooked this I used lemon thyme from my window-box and it was gorgeous – the thyme complements the flavour of trout, which, as far as fish goes, has quite an earthy, gamey taste. In the supermarkets on the whole you can only get farmed trout, which isn't bad and is very good value. However, they are starting to get some better stuff now, like sea-reared trout, which means that they put the trout in pens out in the sea so that the fish can eat some real food and swim against real currents; I think this improves their flavour slightly. Supermarkets also sell some very nicely filleted trout, which are completely boneless, very easy and quick to prepare and good for home use. The best place to buy fish must always be your local fishmonger, who should be able to get hold of wild trout. Alternatively, go fishing and catch your own.

Serves 4
4 × 455g/1lb trout, scaled and gutted (ask your fishmonger)
2 good handfuls of fresh thyme, picked
Maldon salt and freshly ground black pepper
3 tablespoons olive oil
2 lemons
4 bay leaves, fresh if possible

Preheat your oven to its highest temperature. Wash the trout inside and out and pat dry with kitchen paper. Using a pestle and mortar, smash up the thyme with 1 teaspoon of Maldon salt and the olive oil (or very finely chop). Rub this mixture into the trout; smear the flavour into the belly cavity and onto the skin.

Cut the lemons in half and remove the ends so they have a flat edge. With the point of a knife, make an incision into the flesh of each lemon half and stick a bay leaf into it. Place the trout and lemons on a roasting tray and bake in the oven, allowing roughly 10 minutes. To check that the trout is cooked properly, just go to the thickest part of the trout fillet and try to pull the meat away from the bone. If it pulls away easily it is cooked, and if it doesn't put it back into the oven for a couple more minutes. By the time the trout has

finished cooking the skin should be crispy. The roasted lemons should be beautifully sweet and slightly jammy in flavour – this is such a nice way to cook the lemons as the bay also infuses its flavour.

Serve the trout with the lemon, which you can squeeze on to the fish. I like to serve this with some sauté potatoes and a crisp green salad.

Baked Red Mullet with Oregano, Lemon and Black Olive Mash

Red mullet are very plentiful in our waters and are easily obtainable, so there is no excuse for them not being fresh. You can cook them whole, or ask your fishmonger to scale, fillet and pinbone them. I also like to use this recipe for sea bass, sea bream and John Dory. It's simple, fresh and has a delicate flavour.

Serves 4
4 fillets of red mullet
½ clove of garlic
salt and freshly ground black pepper
1 handful of fresh oregano, picked
2 tablespoons olive oil
juice of ½ lemon
black olive mash (see page 141)

Score the skin side of the fillets across at an angle, so that the marinade can penetrate the fish. In a pestle and mortar smash up the garlic, then add a teaspoon of salt and the oregano. Pound this up to a pulp (or very finely chop) and stir in the olive oil and the juice of ½ a lemon. Smear this all over the fillets. This amount should just cover all the fillets (you don't want them swimming in the marinade!). Lay the fillets on a clean baking tray, skin side up. Place at the top of a hot oven (highest temperature) and roast for about 7 minutes (cooking at the top of the oven helps to make the skin nice and crispy). Take care not to overcook the fish.

Serve the mullet beside the black olive mash, with a simple green salad.

John Dory Baked in a Bag with Marinated Cherry Tomatoes, Black Olives and Basil

You can buy John Dory in supermarkets and fishmongers pretty much all year round. I think it's a really wicked fish; when raw the flesh is dense and waxy, and when cooked it feels meaty. It's a great carrier of flavours, so you can pretty much cook it in any way and with anything you like.

This is a really nice way to cook John Dory – it's so Mediterranean and makes you feel as if you are eating abroad. And it tastes superb. The secret is to get the freshest John Dory and the best black olives you can find.

Serves 4
4 John Dory fillets, scaled (each about 225g/8oz in weight)
salt and freshly ground black pepper
4 tablespoons olive oil
2 glasses dry white wine

Marinade
1 good handful of your favourite black olives, stoned
1 clove of garlic, peeled and finely chopped
½ small dried red chilli
1 good handful of fresh basil or marjoram or both, picked and roughly chopped
2–3 tablespoons of your best extra virgin olive oil
20 cherry tomatoes, halved or quartered
1 lemon
salt and freshly ground black pepper

First make the marinade for the tomatoes. Put the olives into a bowl with the garlic, chilli, herbs and oil. Add the cherry tomatoes. I like to leave the marinade for about ½ hour before I season it, as the juice from the tomatoes helps to bring out the excess salt in the olives. Add the lemon juice and seasoning to taste. This marinade keeps for about a day. You can add sun-dried tomatoes to intensify the tomato flavour.

Take a piece of kitchen foil approximately 40cm/15 inches in length. Place a quarter of the marinated ingredients in the centre of the right-hand half, with one of your seasoned John Dory fillets on top. Fold over the left-hand half and seal two sides by folding over tightly to gently hug the fish. Add 1 tablespoon of olive oil and a quarter of the white wine, and seal up the remaining side. Repeat the process for the remaining 3 fillets. Bake in the oven at its highest temperature for approximately 10 minutes. Remove from the oven and allow to stand for 3–4 minutes without opening the bag.

To serve, place an unopened bag on each plate and let your guests open them up and remove the contents themselves.

Seared Encrusted Tuna Steak with Fresh Coriander and Basil

Tuna is widely available in supermarkets and fishmongers these days. There are many types: the best sushi/sushini quality tuna is blue-fin tuna, and big-eye tuna is a very close second best. These two types of tuna can be bought in Britain but are very expensive, as most of it is bought for the Japanese market, where they prize it like gold. The most available and reasonably priced is yellow-fin tuna, which can be pretty good. When buying tuna you should look for meat that is evenly coloured, dark red and has a fine, tight grain free of large sinews. Generally you get better tuna in good fishmongers than in supermarkets, but sometimes the supermarkets get a good batch in, so keep your eyes peeled. There is a bit of a thing about it being fashionable to serve tuna pink; if you buy good-quality fresh tuna the last thing you want to do is cook it all the way through and make it taste like tinned tuna, so yes, good-quality fresh tuna *should* be served rare or very pink.

Serves 4
1 small dried red chilli
1 tablespoon coriander seeds
½ clove of garlic
1 good handful of basil, picked and finely chopped
1 good handful of fresh coriander, picked and finely chopped
salt and freshly ground black pepper
juice of 1 lemon
4 tuna steaks, 225–285g/8–10oz each, about 2cm/¾ inch thick

Smash up the chilli and the coriander seeds in a pestle and mortar. Add the garlic, basil, coriander and lemon juice to taste. Mix together, and season.

Lay out your tuna steaks on a tray, season both sides and rub the herb mixture on to each side.

There are two nice ways to cook it: I prefer to cook it on one of those ridged grill pans or in a frying-pan. Rub your pan, which should be very, very hot, with a little bit of oil on a piece of kitchen paper, then put in the tuna. What you want to do is sear the tuna so that it toasts, fries and browns (about 45–60 seconds on each side). Once cooked, I like to rip the steaks in half and serve with salad and chips or boiled potatoes and a big wedge of lemon. It's quite sexy sometimes with some marinated sun-dried tomatoes, olives, basil . . . the possibilities are endless.

Quick Marinated Whole Roasted Bream with Balsamic Vinegar and Crispy Marjoram

Red bream and royal bream are easily and cheaply available at all fishmongers and supermarkets these days. Ask your fishmonger to gut and scale the bream if it has not been done already. You could even ask him to fillet it for you if you don't like bones. Bream is an interesting fish to eat, as it is quite flaky and very delicate in flavour. I think the sweetness of the balsamic vinegar and marjoram works extremely well with the bream.

Serves 4
2 × 455g/1lb red or royal bream
½ clove of garlic, finely chopped
1 good handful of fresh basil or marjoram, picked
salt and freshly ground black pepper
150ml/10 tablespoons balsamic vinegar
4 tablespoons olive oil
extra garlic and marjoram for garnish

Preheat the oven and roasting tray at the highest temperature. Wash the bream inside and out and pat dry with kitchen paper. Lay them on a board and score at an angle, criss-cross fashion, about 2cm/¾ inch apart, so that it looks a little bit like noughts and crosses – do this on both sides (if filleted do the same, but don't score quite as deep). Pound or finely chop the garlic and basil, or marjoram, with a teaspoon of salt and stir in your balsamic vinegar and olive oil. Smear and rub this inside and outside your bream, especially into the scorings, with a twist of pepper. Leave for 10 minutes. Place the fish, and any extra marinade, on a lightly oiled tray and roast for about 12 minutes. Leave to rest for 1 minute, allowing all the lovely milky juices to relax back into the flesh. To check that the fish is cooked, try to pull away the thickest part of the fillet from the bone. If it comes away easily it is done. Fry off some thinly sliced garlic and marjoram leaves until crisp and sprinkle over the fish. Serve with roasted cherry tomatoes, boiled potatoes and a salad.

Tray-baked Salmon with Olives, Green Beans, Anchovies and Tomatoes

The idea of this dish is to bake your salmon plainly with a little olive oil and sea salt. In the same tray, bake tomatoes, olives and blanched green beans, laying anchovies over the beans. As the anchovies cook they fall apart, and as the olives roast they sort of infuse a smoky flavour with the tomatoes. This is a really choice combination – you must try it.

Serves 4
200g/7oz green beans
20 small cherry tomatoes
1–2 good handfuls of black olives
2 tablespoons extra virgin olive oil
salt and freshly ground black pepper
4 × 225g/8oz thick salmon fillet steaks, with or without skin
    but definitely pinboned
2 lemons
1 handful of fresh basil, picked
12 anchovy fillets

First of all tail the green beans, blanch them until tender in salted, boiling water, and drain. Put in a bowl with the cherry tomatoes and the stoned olives. Toss in the olive oil and a pinch of salt and pepper.

Give the salmon fillets a quick wash under the tap and pat dry with kitchen paper. Squeeze the juice of ½ a lemon over the fillets, on both sides, then season both sides with salt and pepper and drizzle a little olive oil over the top. Preheat the oven and a roasting tray at the highest temperature. Put your 4 fillets of salmon at one end of the roasting tray. Toss the basil into the green beans, olives and tomatoes and place this mixture at the other end of the tray. Lay the anchovies over the green beans. Roast in the preheated oven for 10 minutes, then remove from the oven and serve with lemon quarters.

This is very tasty with some homemade mayonnaise or aïoli (see page 229).

Fresh sardines are something really special; they taste lovely and are cheap and highly nutritious. They are definitely underrated. Whole grilled or baked sardines are beautiful, but I am giving you a recipe that's a bit different and classy, the filling going in the direction of a kind of panzanella. When buying always look for shiny, glassy-eyed, pleasant-smelling sardines.

Preparation

Scrape the scales from the fish with a knife (try not to cut the skin). Cut off the head, slit open the belly and remove the innards under cold running water. Open out the inside of the sardine just like a book, press and flatten the sides down with your thumbs. Pull out the backbone from the head end to the tail.

Stuffed, Rolled and Baked Sardines with Pine Nuts and Fresh Herbs

Serves 4
4 plum tomatoes
12 large sardines, prepared (see opposite)
zest and juice of 1 lemon
salt and freshly ground black pepper
1 medium onion, peeled and finely chopped
4 tablespoons olive oil
1 clove of garlic
1 bulb of fennel, trimmed and finely chopped, saving any green tops
1 small red chilli, pounded
1 handful of fresh basil, finely chopped
1 handful of fresh parsley, finely chopped
3 handfuls of breadcrumbs (equivalent to 6 slices of bread)
1 good handful of pine nuts
extra virgin olive oil for drizzling

Score the tomatoes and blanch in boiling water. Remove the skins, deseed and chop finely. Lay out the sardines in a dish and sprinkle with the finely grated lemon zest, then squeeze the lemon juice over them. Season lightly with salt and pepper. Gently and slowly sweat the onion in the olive oil with a pinch of salt in a thick-bottomed frying-pan. After about 3 minutes, add the garlic and cook without colouring for another minute. Add the fennel and cook for 1 minute more, just to slightly soften the fennel, then transfer the contents of the pan to a bowl and allow to cool. Add the tomatoes, chilli, herbs and breadcrumbs and stir.

Sprinkle a little of the mixture in the bottom of an oil-rubbed earthenware-type dish, into which the rolled fillets will fit, then, one by one, pat a little more of the mixture on each fillet and roll up like a swiss roll. Place in the dish, sprinkle the remaining herb mixture, the pine nuts and fennel tops on top, drizzle with olive oil and bake in a hot oven (highest temperature) for 8–10 minutes until crisp and golden. Great for lunch, dinner or a snack.

Fish in Sea Salt

Fish cooked this way is so quick and easy, dead sociable to eat and, most importantly, tastes luscious. The fish retains all its natural moisture and juices and just seems to melt away from the bone; it does not, as you would imagine, taste salty at all.

I use whole fish, which means you can cook a small mullet or John Dory for 1 or 2 people or cook a large salmon, bass or brill for a group or party. My favourite fish for this method of cooking are red mullet, bream, salmon, turbot, brill and trout. Ask your fishmonger to scale and gut the fish, then all you have to do is stuff the belly cavity with fresh fragrant herbs and lemon slices. Choose a selection of fresh herbs – basil, flat-leaf parsley, fennel tops, dill, coriander or bay. Then take an appropriately sized baking tray and lay baking foil over it, allowing an extra 30cm/12 inches to hang over each side. Sprinkle at least 2cm/¾in of coarse sea salt on the bottom – you can buy large kilogram bags of coarse sea salt (it must be coarse, unground sea salt) in supermarkets. Place your whole stuffed fish on top of the salt (I always make sure that there are enough herbs hanging/bulging out of the belly cavity to stop the salt getting in). Sprinkle the rest of the salt on top (about 2cm/¾in high). Then just crumple up the excess foil and push down between the salt and the tray (this basically just hugs the fish at the sides and saves you having to use too much salt). Drizzle a little water over the top of the salt to help make a crust. Cook in the middle of the oven at its highest temperature for 10 minutes per 450g/1lb.

If you are cooking wild salmon you might want to undercook it slightly to appreciate its clean and natural taste. Simply reduce the cooking time by 2 minutes per 450g/1lb (wild salmon is probably the only fish that I would do this with).

After baking allow to rest for 15 minutes (the fish will carry on gently cooking), then gently break and remove the salt; be careful not to pierce the skin of the fish as you will make the flesh salty. After exposing the lovely steaming fish, simply place it in the middle of the table with some fresh bread, crisp green salad, boiled potatoes and two or three dips.

Kedgeree

This is such a versatile dish, wonderful for breakfast, or for lunch or supper. This recipe is an excellent balance between smoky and spicy.

Serves 6
2 eggs
680g/1½lb undyed smoked haddock fillets, pinboned
2 bay leaves
170g/6oz long-grain or basmati rice
salt and freshly ground black pepper
115g/4oz butter
1 medium onion or equivalent spring onions, finely chopped
1 clove of garlic, finely chopped
2 heaped teaspoons curry powder
2 lemons
2 good handfuls of fresh coriander, roughly chopped

Boil the eggs for 10 minutes and leave them in cold water until they're needed. Put the haddock in a frying-pan with some water and the bay leaves, bring to the boil, cover and simmer for about 5 minutes until the fish is cooked. Remove from the pan and, when cool enough to handle, remove the skin, flake the fish into chunks and set aside.

Cook the rice in salted water for about 10 minutes then drain. Refresh in cold water, drain again and leave it in the fridge until you need it. Melt the butter in a pan over a low heat and add the onion and garlic. Allow to soften without colouring for about 5 minutes, then add the curry powder and cook for a couple of minutes more. Add the juice of 1 lemon. Cut the hard-boiled eggs into wedges. Add the fish and the rice to the pan and gently heat through, then add the eggs and coriander, and stir in gently. Put into a warm serving dish and serve with the second lemon, cut into wedges – you'll love it!

Perfectly Cooked Live Lobster

You can buy ready-cooked lobsters in the supermarkets for quite a reasonable price, but to experience the sublime flavour of lobster as it should be, you must buy your lobsters live and cook them yourself. You won't get them any fresher than that. You will probably have to order them from your fishmonger or supermarket in advance. They will be blackish but will turn bright red during cooking.

It's nice to buy one lobster weighing about 1100g/2½lb, for 2 people, or smaller ones for each person. Ask your fishmonger what sizes he has available. Your lobster will have its pincers secured with rubber bands – just leave these on until it is cooked.

Take the lobster home and place a wet towel over it – the darkness will make it go to sleep. You can either cook it in well-salted water (as salty as sea water – Rick Stein actually cooks his lobsters in sea water) or you can make a fragrant broth with celery, fennel, chillies, bay and other herbs.

Fill a large pan with enough water to cover the lobster, then, only when the water is boiling fast, put it in head first and cover with a lid. Cook for about 3 minutes per 455g/1lb. Remove from the pan and allow to rest for 5 minutes. Now you need a good sharp knife (a serrated one is good). Place the lobster on a board, its tail facing away from you. There is a line running along its back to its head. Just behind its eyes, place the point of your knife and split down to the front end, then turn it round and split down to the other end, so that you have cut along the lobster's entire length. Remove the dark intestinal vein that runs down the tail, the small stomach sac, which lies in the head, and the gills. (If the lobster is to be served cold, allow it to cool in its shell to keep the flesh moist.) Crack open the claws with the base of a large cook's knife. Serve flesh side up.

Lobster is such a sociable thing to eat. I always serve it simply, with an interesting green salad, fresh bread, and two or three homemade dips or sauces such as lemon or basil mayonnaise, aïoli, chilli and fennel salsa, sweet chilli and pepper salsa (see pages 229, 234, 235). Put a finger-bowl on the table and serve some cold and crisp white wine.

NB In my opinion it is not necessary to kill the lobster with a knife before cooking (as some people do) because it will die instantly when plunged into the boiling water and unless you kill it properly with the knife it could end up in pain. Also, I believe that by piercing the lobster the meat will not taste as good because a lot of the succulent juices will have been allowed to escape into the water. Sorry if this all sounds a bit harsh.

MEAT, POULTRY
AND GAME

Pork Chops with Thyme, Lemon and Pesto

Regular cut pork chops will do for this recipe, but when I make this dish I ask my butcher to cut a two-rib chop, lose one of the ribs, trim off the excess fat and bat it out slightly – now that's a real chop! A good butcher won't mind doing this. The chops are probably best cooked on a ridged griddle, but you can pan-fry or roast them.

Serves 4
1 handful of thyme, picked
salt and freshly ground black pepper
1 clove of garlic
zest and juice of 1 lemon
1 tablespoon olive oil
4 two-rib pork loin chops, or regular chops
1 pesto recipe (see page 232)

Using a pestle and mortar pound, or very finely chop, the thyme with 1 teaspoon of salt. When pulped, add the garlic and 1 teaspoon of black pepper and pound again. Stir in the lemon juice and zest and the olive oil. Smear the mixture over the chops and leave for at least 10 minutes.

Place the chops on a very hot griddle or in a hot frying-pan (they make a bit of smoke, so get your fan on!). Try to get each side nicely charred and golden, but take care and don't let them burn; if it looks as if they are getting too much colour, turn the heat down. They take about 8 minutes to cook at a medium high heat. Don't overcook pork, it isn't necessary and will only make the meat dry. Rest the chops for a few minutes, then spoon some pesto over them.

Serve with a mixed salad and mashed or jacket potatoes, rubbed with olive oil and rolled in sea salt and baked.

Pork and Crackling

If you have a good butcher, ask him for the rib or rump end of the pork loin – it's more evenly-sized, making it easier to cook. Ask him to leave the skin on and to score it across with lines about 5mm/¼in apart and then to take it off the bone. Ask him to chop the bones up for you and take them home to use for your gravy.

Serves 8
½ pork loin roughly 3kg/7lb in weight (on the bone)
Maldon sea salt
1 tablespoon chopped fresh rosemary
½ tablespoon fennel seeds
5 cloves of garlic
8 tablespoons balsamic vinegar
4 bay leaves
2 tablespoons olive oil
pork bones, chopped
5 outer sticks of celery, roughly chopped
1 large carrot, roughly chopped
1 large onion, roughly chopped

Lay out your pork on a board and rub some salt and chopped rosemary into the scored lines, trying to get this into every bit by pushing and rubbing in. In a pestle and mortar smash up the fennel seeds, then the garlic and remaining chopped rosemary, and rub this into the meat – not the skin, or it will burn. Place in a large roasting tray with the balsamic vinegar, bay and olive oil. Leave for about ½ hour to marinate.

Meanwhile, preheat your oven to its highest temperature and brown the bones. Rub the skin of the pork with lots of sea salt – this will help puff it up and dry it out. Place the pork directly on to the bars at the top of the oven. Finally add the browned bones and vegetables to the left-over balsamic marinade, add 570ml/1 pint water and put into the oven directly under the pork. As the pork cooks all the goodness drips from it into the tray. This liquid will then become your gravy. You also get quite nice charred bar marks on the base of the pork.

The pork will take about 1 hour to cook. After 20 minutes turn the temperature down to 220°C/425°F/gas 7. Once the pork is cooked, remove it from the oven on the rack and place on a piece of foil to save any juices. Allow to rest for at least 10 minutes. Finish off any vegetables that you are going to serve with it and make a gravy out of the juices in the tray which was underneath the pork.

Gravy

Put the bones, the liquid and the vegetables into a large pan. Add some water to the tray that contained the bones and vegetables, as there will be some Marmite-like, sticky stuff on the bottom of the tray which is very tasty. Reboil the water, scrape off all the goodness from the bottom of the tray and then pour everything into the pan. Bring to the boil, shaking occasionally, remove any oil, grease or scum from the top, then pass the contents through a sieve, discarding all the vegetables and bones. You can reduce and then correct the seasoning to taste.

North African Lamb with Chilli, Ginger, Chickpeas and Couscous

This is a great dish. It's fun to cook and it has a really authentic flavour. The fragrant warmth of the chillies and ginger really make this one. I use trimmed neck fillet of lamb (or you could use any nice stewing lamb), which is widely available in supermarkets and is reasonably priced.

Serves 4–6

170g/6oz chickpeas, soaked overnight

2 large firm aubergines

salt and freshly ground black pepper

10 fresh plum tomatoes

1½ tablespoons coriander seeds

½ teaspoon cumin seeds

grated nutmeg to taste

4 neck fillets of lamb (285g/10oz each),
    sliced into 5cm/2 inch pieces

4 tablespoons olive oil

4 medium/large chillies, chopped

2 tablespoons grated fresh ginger

2 cloves of garlic, finely chopped

1 teaspoon vinegar

2 tablespoons chopped fresh parsley

1 tablespoon chopped fresh coriander

couscous (see recipes pages 180–81)

Drain the soaked chickpeas. Cover with water, bring to the boil and cook until tender. Chop the aubergines into rough, chunky 2.5cm/1-inch-size dice and place in a colander over the sink. Sprinkle with salt (about 1 tablespoon). This will dehydrate the aubergines and drain away some of the bitter juices (leave for about ½ hour). Blanch the tomatoes in boiling water, remove the skins, deseed and quarter.

Using a pestle and mortar, pound up the coriander seeds, cumin seeds and 1 teaspoon salt, then put into a bowl and add 12 gratings of nutmeg. Toss the lamb into the mixture and stir well to coat. Heat a large casserole pan, add 2 tablespoons of olive oil and sear the lamb until dark golden brown.

Gently squeeze the excess liquid from the aubergines (this will take away most of the salt too). Add 2 more tablespoons of olive oil to your hot pan and fry the aubergines with the lamb for about 2 minutes, keeping everything on the move. Add the chilli and ginger and cook for 3 minutes. Then add the garlic and cook for 1 minute (still stirring, so as not to over-colour). Add the vinegar and tomatoes and shake now and again. Turn the heat down to a gentle simmer, place a lid on and leave for 1 hour, then add the cooked chickpeas and simmer for a further 5 minutes. The tomatoes should have melted to a sauce and the aubergines should be sweet. Check the seasoning and stir in the parsley and coriander. Serve with couscous.

Roast Leg of Lamb

A leg of lamb (about 2kg/4–5lb) is always a real treat, and I like to try different ways of enhancing its wonderful flavour. Here are a few of my favourite ways to add something to a roast.

On the whole, lamb is good nearly all year round, and although early spring lamb is lovely and tender, in my opinion it's at its best around May, when the meat of the spring lamb has had time to develop flavour, character, texture and basically tastes like lamb should.

A leg of lamb should be soft to the touch and leave a slight indent when pressed. The skin should be dry, but not cracking or flaking. Ask your butcher to remove the bottom socket joint to make cooking and carving easier.

Cooking Times

Pink – 10 minutes for every 450g/1lb plus 20 minutes
Medium – 13 minutes for every 450g/1lb plus 20 minutes
Well-done – 20 minutes for every 450g/1lb plus 20 minutes

Always rest the meat for at least 10 minutes before carving.

Roast Leg of Lamb with Anchovies and Rosemary

1 leg of lamb (about 2kg/4½lb)
½ lemon
1 handful of rosemary, roughly chopped
10 fillets of salted anchovies or anchovies in oil
salt and freshly ground black pepper
olive oil

With a sharp pointed knife, pierce the skin of the lamb at an angle about 5cm/2 inches deep and about 10 times randomly about the leg, poking your finger into each cut to make a bit more room. Rub the skin with the lemon and push the rosemary into the cuts and on to the skin. Stuff the anchovy fillets into the cuts. Season the outside of the lamb with salt and pepper. Put a little oil into a roasting tray (preferably a thick one) and add the lamb. Roast it in the oven at 225°C/425°F/gas 7, turning every 30 minutes until cooked.

Roast Leg of Lamb with Rosemary and Garlic

1 leg of lamb (about 2kg/4½lb)
½ lemon
1 handful of picked fresh rosemary
salt
1 clove of garlic
olive oil
some extra branches of fresh rosemary

Slice off small pieces of skin about the size of a 10p piece at random around the leg of lamb. Lightly rub with the lemon. With a knife, follow the bone down about 10–12cm/4 inches (you are just making a 'tunnel' where you are cutting the meat away from the bone). Do this from the top end and the bottom end. Using a pestle and mortar, smash up a small handful of picked rosemary with 1 teaspoon salt. Add the garlic and ½ tablespoon of olive oil and pound again. Rub this mixture on to the exposed flesh and push into the gaps you have made with the knife next to the bone. This will infuse a great fragrance. Season the skin with salt, and then sprinkle it with rosemary. Tie lots of branches of rosemary around the meat. Put a little oil in a hot roasting tray (preferably a nice thick one), add the lamb, and roast it in the oven at 225°C/425°F/gas 7, turning every 30 minutes.

Roast Leg of Lamb with Pancetta, Sage and Rosemary

1 leg of lamb (about 2kg/4½lb)
1 handful of fresh sage
1 clove of garlic
salt and freshly ground black pepper
juice of 1 lemon
olive oil
1 handful of fresh rosemary
85g/3oz pancetta, sliced

With a knife, follow the lamb bone down about 10–12cm/4 inches (you are just making a 'tunnel' where you are cutting the meat away from the bone). Do this from the top end and the bottom end. Pierce the skin at an angle with a sharp pointed knife 6 or 8 times at random around the leg. Where you have made the incisions, open them up a bit by poking your fingers down them to make a bit of space.

Using a pestle and mortar smash up half the sage with the garlic and 1 teaspoon of salt. When it's pulped, add the lemon juice, 2 tablespoons of olive oil, the other half of the sage and the rosemary, roughly chopped. Stuff the mixture into all the incisions and gaps you have made with the knife. Then stuff the pancetta deep into the gaps along the bone and the incisions. This gives a lovely fragrant flavour to the meat. Put a little oil in a hot roasting tray (preferably a nice thick one), add the lamb, and roast it in the oven at 225°C/425°F/gas 7 turning every 30 minutes until cooked.

Roast Leg of Lamb with Apricot and Thyme

1 leg of lamb (about 2kg/4½lb)
1 handful of picked thyme
½ clove garlic
salt
olive oil
juice of ½ lemon
1 handful of dried apricots

With a knife, follow the lamb bone down about 10–12cm/4 inches (you are just making a 'tunnel' where you are cutting the meat away from the bone). Do this from the top end and the bottom end. Pierce the skin at an angle with a sharp pointed knife 6 or 8 times at random around the leg. Where you have made the incisions, open them up a bit by poking your fingers down them to make a bit of space. Using a pestle and mortar, smash up a good handful of thyme leaves with the garlic and 1 teaspoon of salt. When it's pulped, add 1 tablespoon olive oil and the juice of ½ a lemon.

Roughly chop up a good handful of dried apricots (these taste great) and mix up with what's in the pestle and mortar. Stuff all of this into all the incisions and gaps that you have made with the knife. Rub any excess over the skin. Season with a little salt. Put a little oil in a hot roasting tray (preferably a nice thick one), add the lamb, then roast it in the oven at 225°C/425°F/gas 7, turning every 30 minutes until cooked.

Spiced Slow-cooked Lamb Shanks

This is one of the cheapest and tastiest cuts of lamb. Cooked this way, the sauce is very tasty and the meat will just fall off the bone. Served with potato mash, polenta, couscous or rice, it is a wonderful dish.

Serves 4
4 lamb shanks
sea salt and freshly ground black pepper
1 teaspoon coriander seeds
1 small dried red chilli (or 2 teaspoons chopped fresh chilli)
1 tablespoon fresh rosemary
1 teaspoon dried marjoram or oregano
1 tablespoon flour
1 tablespoon olive oil
1 clove of garlic, finely chopped
1 large carrot, quartered and finely sliced
6 sticks of celery, quartered and finely sliced
2 medium/large onions, quartered and finely chopped
2 tablespoons balsamic vinegar
170ml/6fl oz dry white wine
6 anchovy fillets
2 × 400g/14oz tins of plum tomatoes
1 handful of fresh basil, marjoram or flat-leaf parsley, roughly chopped

Season the lamb with sea salt and freshly ground black pepper. Smash up the coriander seeds and dried chilli and mix with the chopped rosemary and dried marjoram. Roll the lamb in this mixture, pressing it in well. Dust the lamb with the flour.

Heat a thick-bottomed casserole pan, add the oil, brown the meat on all sides and then remove from the pan. Add the garlic, carrot, celery, onions and a pinch of salt and sweat them until softened. Add the balsamic vinegar and allow it to reduce to a syrup. Pour in the white wine and allow to simmer for 2 minutes. Add the anchovies (these really seem to intensify the lamb flavour) and then add the tinned tomatoes, kept whole. Shake the pan and return the lamb to it. Bring to the boil, put on the lid and simmer in the oven at 180°C/350°F/gas 5 for 1½ hours, then remove the lid and cook for a further ½ hour. Skim off any fat and taste for seasoning. Finally, stir in a handful of roughly chopped fresh basil, marjoram or flat-leaf parsley.

My Perfect Roast Chicken

I cook this every week and I always try to do something different with it. I've never actually seen anyone cook it like this but it's very straightforward – it must be the best way to have roast chicken and it makes a real change. Basically what I do is carefully part the skin from the meat on the top of the chicken breast and stuff the gap with fresh, delicate herbs such as parsley, basil and marjoram. Then I tie it up and roast it with some olive oil and salt.

Serves 4
1.1–1.4kg/2½–3lb free-range chicken
salt and freshly ground black pepper
3 small handfuls of fresh herbs (basil, parsley, marjoram),
  picked and finely chopped
4 tablespoons olive oil
1 lemon, halved
4 bay leaves, torn
2 sprigs of fresh rosemary

Preheat the oven and a roasting tray to 225°C/425°F/gas 7. Wash the chicken inside and out and pat it as dry as possible with kitchen paper. Some people remove the wishbone but I like to leave it in and make a wish. Rub the cavity with salt, then, being very careful, grab the skin at the tip of the chicken breasts, making sure that it doesn't rip, and pull up gently. With your other hand gently separate the skin from the meat of the breast. It's normally connected by a little bit of tissuey-type stuff, and you can either leave this attached in the middle and make two little tunnels either side or you can try to cut away the middle. Sprinkle a little salt down the gaps that you have made, and push in the chopped herbs. Drizzle in a little olive oil. I don't always stuff the chicken but when I do I generally go with lemon, bay and

rosemary, which I push into the cavity at this point. Pull the skin of the chicken breast forward so that none of the actual flesh is exposed, tuck the little winglets under, and tie up as firmly as possible.

To me the perfect roast chicken has tender moist breast meat, crisp skin and, dare I say it, over-cooked thigh meat. So at this point, simply slash across each thigh about 3 or 4 times and rub in some of the leftover herbs, which allows the heat to penetrate directly into the thigh meat, enabling it to cook faster. With your hand, rub a little olive oil into the skin of the chicken and season very generously with salt and pepper. Remove the hot tray from the oven and add a little oil. Put the chicken, breast side down, on the bottom of the tray and put back into the oven. Allow to cook for 5 minutes, then turn it over on to the other side, breast side down. Cook for another 5 minutes and then place the chicken on its bottom. Cook for 1 hour at 225°C/425°F/gas 7.

Use any excess fat that drips off into the roasting tray to roast your potatoes, or cook the potatoes in the tray with your chicken. The skin should be really crispy and the herbs will flavour the flesh – this really must be the best roast chicken. Trust me – it's not fiddly, it's pukka.

Fragrant Green Chicken Curry

I was asked to make this by my sister's husband, who'd eaten something similar in a Thai restaurant. I looked up a lot of recipes and they all seemed quite different, so I used them as a basis and added some more fresh herbs, trying to get it as fragrant as possible. If you are a veggie, replace the chicken with vegetables of your choice.

Serves 4
4 chicken breasts without bone and skin, each cut into 5 large pieces
1 × 400ml tin of coconut milk
1 handful of chopped pistachio nuts

Green curry paste
6 spring onions, washed and trimmed
4–6 medium green chillies, deseeded and finely chopped
2 cloves of garlic
1 tablespoon fresh root ginger, peeled and finely chopped
1 tablespoon coriander seeds, pounded or crushed
½ teaspoon freshly ground black pepper
Maldon sea salt and freshly ground black pepper, to taste

half a handful of lime leaves, torn
2 lemon grass stalks, trimmed back and finely chopped
2 good handfuls of fresh basil on the stalk
3 good handfuls of fresh coriander on the stalk
3 tablespoons extra virgin olive oil
zest and juice of 4 limes

Put all the green curry paste ingredients in a food processor and whizz to a smooth green paste. Marinate the chicken in a little of the paste for 30 minutes, then add a little oil and the chicken pieces to a hot casserole-type pan or wok. Fry for 4 minutes, then add the remainder of the marinade – it will sizzle and spit. Stir in the coconut milk, bring to the boil and simmer gently for 8 minutes until the chicken is cooked. Season to taste. The flavour should have a kick but be reasonably mellow – very fresh and fragrant.

Sprinkle with the pistachios and some coriander leaves and serve with steamed rice or noodles, and chunky coconut, tomato, cucumber and lime relish (see page 236).

The Most Perfect Steamed and Roasted Duck with Honey and Oyster Sauce

There are a lot of recipes for cooking duck but this is an absolutely superb way to have it and lends itself to several different ways of serving it. You can roast the duck and serve it whole with roasted vegetables and gravy (see below). You can strip the duck off the bone, like they do in Chinatown, and serve it with spring onions, cucumber, little Chinese pancakes and plum sauce. Or you can eat it cold with a salad the next day. As we all know, the trick is to make the skin crispy.

Serves 4
4 good tablespoons fragrant honey
8 tablespoons oyster sauce
2 × 680–900g/1½–2lb Gressingham or Barbary ducks
2 sticks of celery, thinly sliced
4 spring onions, roughly chopped
6 cloves of garlic, peeled and squashed
4 bay leaves
1 handful of basil and coriander, torn
1 medium fresh red chilli, thinly sliced
salt and freshly ground black pepper

Preheat your oven to 225°C/425°F/gas 7. Make your sauce by putting the honey and oyster sauce into a pan and heat slightly. Now prepare each duck by pulling away any excess fat from within its cavity. Wash inside and out and pat dry with some kitchen paper. Put all your vegetables, garlic, herbs and chilli in a bowl, mix with 2 good pinches of salt and black pepper, and toss. Stuff your ducks with this filling.

Place the ducks on a rack (not vital but it helps) inside a roasting tray. Add roughly 565ml/1 pint of boiling water to the bottom of the tray, tightly cover the tray and the ducks with tinfoil, and place in the oven for 1 hour. This will steam the ducks and will start to bring the fat out of the skin. After 1 hour carefully remove the ducks from the oven and remove the tinfoil, being careful not to burn yourself. Then, pushing away from you with the back of a knife, gently rub and push the skin of the duck. You'll see loads of fat being pushed out of the skin as you do this. Let this drip into the roasting tray and then pour all of the fluid at the bottom of the tray into a bowl, where it will separate. Use the fat on the top to roast potatoes and use the stock at the bottom to make a gravy or sauce later on (see below). Brush the ducks all over with the honey and oyster sauce – this will coat and cook into the skin giving it a dark colour and a great flavour.

Put the ducks back into the oven, being careful not to let the skin burn or catch (by the way don't watch it burn – cover with foil or turn the heat down if it is colouring too much), turning as frequently as you care to. Brush every 10 minutes with the honey and oyster sauce. Remove the ducks from the oven after 40 minutes, and allow to rest while you make the gravy. By the time the ducks have finished cooking the meat should be cooked all the way through (not pink) and the skin should be crisp and thin, having rendered most of the fat away.

Gravy

Remove excess fat from the roasting tray and place the tray on the hob. Cook gently to reduce any leftover liquor to a syrup. Shake out the stuffing from the duck and add to the tray with the separated stock (reserved earlier). (If you feel it's appropriate you could pour in a good glass of wine at this stage – allowing it to cook out for 1 minute before adding the stock.) Stir and reduce by half, making sure that all the goodness has dissolved into the gravy. Pour the liquid through a sieve into a small pan, allow to stand, and then skim. Season if necessary.

Pot-roasted Guinea Fowl with Sage, Celery and Blood Orange

This is a gorgeous recipe. The guinea fowl is cooked slowly in a pot, so it combines braising and roasting. The richness of the butter, used to baste the birds, with sage and garlic, works superbly with the guinea fowl. The fresh and fragrant flavours of the orange, thyme and celery, used to stuff the guinea fowl, steam in the cavity, infusing their flavour into the breast meat. The stuffing is also great as a chunky and tasty addition to your gravy (see page 128).

Serves 4–6
2 × 900–1100g/2–2½lb guinea fowl
8 blood oranges
1 bulb of celery
1 small handful fresh thyme, picked
Maldon sea salt and freshly ground black pepper
1 tablespoon olive oil
6 cloves of garlic, whole and unpeeled
85g/3oz butter
10 sage leaves
350ml/12fl oz fruity dry white wine

Remove any excess fat from the cavity of each guinea fowl. Wash thoroughly inside and out and pat dry with kitchen paper. Rub the cavity with a little salt. Cut off the two ends of the oranges, stand them on end and carefully slice off the skin (once you have removed one piece of skin you can see where the flesh meets the skin). Slice the oranges into five or six rounds each. Remove the tougher outside sticks of the celery until you reach the white, dense bulb and slice across thinly. Put in a bowl, mix in the thyme and a small pinch of salt and pepper, then stuff the cavity of each guinea fowl with this filling. Pull the skin at the front of each guinea fowl's cavity forward, to cover the filling, and tightly tie/truss up (see page 120, chicken preparation).

Heat a thick-bottomed pan and add the olive oil and the guinea fowl, the skin of which has been rubbed in Maldon sea salt and pepper. Seal until lightly golden on all sides, then add the garlic, butter and sage and cook for 3–4 minutes until golden brown. Add the wine at intervals, enough to keep the pan slightly moist at all times. Place in the oven at 225°C/425°F/gas 7 for 45 minutes, checking every 10–15 minutes and just topping up the wine as necessary. The guinea fowl will be roasted and semi-steamed.

When cooked, carefully remove from the oven and place upside down on a dish, allowing all the juices and moisture to relax back into the breast meat for at least 5 minutes. While your meat is resting, make the gravy.

Gravy

Remove all the fat from the roasting pan and place the pan on a gentle heat. In the bottom of the pan will be your cooked, soft, sweet, whole garlic cloves and some gorgeous sticky Marmite stuff – when this gets hot, shake out the stuffing from the guinea fowl cavity and add to the pan with a glass of wine. As the wine boils and steams, scrape all the goodness with a spoon from the bottom of the pan into the liquor. When it has all dissolved, leave to simmer gently. Squash the cooked garlic out of the skins with a spoon (discard the skins); this will also thicken the gravy slightly, as well as giving it flavour. Pour any of the juices that have drained out of the rested birds into the pan with the gravy, simmer and season to taste. Serve the guinea fowl with roast potatoes and any simply cooked green vegetable – spinach, curly kale, pak choy or sprouting broccoli.

Pot-roasted Rabbit with Rosemary, Thyme, Sage and Lemon

Rabbit has a subtle and pleasant taste and it's a good carrier of flavours. People tend to associate rabbit with stews or pies, but in this recipe it is pot-roasted quickly.

Serves 2
1 rabbit
1 lemon
salt and freshly ground black pepper
1 heaped tablespoon chopped rosemary
1 heaped tablespoon chopped thyme
1 tablespoon olive oil
1 small and 1 big knob of butter
8 sage leaves
½ clove of garlic, thinly sliced
1 large glass of white wine

For this you'll need a pan or casserole dish that will go on the hob and into the oven. The rabbit should be cut into 4 legs and 4 saddle pieces – your butcher will do this for you, or you can buy it already cut up in the supermarket.

Peel the lemon with a peeler (just to remove the fragrant yellow skin) and roughly slice the peel. Squeeze a little lemon juice over the rabbit joints, just enough to moisten them. Season the pieces generously with salt and pepper and roll them in the rosemary and thyme.

Heat the olive oil in a hot pan, add the rabbit pieces and any remaining rosemary and thyme, and fry them fast for about 5 minutes or until the rabbit is golden brown; about half-way through this process, add the lemon zest, a small knob of butter and the sage leaves (this should make the sage leaves go crispy). Add the garlic and fry for another minute to soften but not colour. Add the white wine, which should sizzle nicely. Finish this in the oven for about 10 minutes at 200°C/400°F/gas 6. Remove from the oven, add a big knob of butter and sloosh it around for a bit. Then allow it to rest for a couple of minutes – the wine and butter should create a lovely mild sauce.

Serve with wedges of roast potato and roasted red onions (see page 153).

Boiled Bacon with Pease Pudding

This always reminds me of my Nan, who often used to cook this when I was a little boy. She cooked the hell out of it in a pressure cooker! It is absolutely delicious, especially with pease pudding and English mustard. You can buy some lovely pieces of gammon or hock bacon from the supermarkets. I always buy the unsmoked bacon for this dish, as it is not such a dominant flavour and you can boil it. Don't forget to soak the split peas the day before.

Serves 6–8

1.4–1.8kg/3–4lb piece of gammon or hock bacon

Stock
2 bay leaves
3 cloves
5 black peppercorns
2 medium onions, roughly chopped
3 medium carrots, roughly chopped
5 sticks celery, roughly chopped

Pease Pudding (see page 161)

Whole Vegetables
12 small carrots, whole
1 trimmed bulb celery, whole
12 small leeks, whole

Check the weight of the joint before you throw away the plastic covering. The cooking time will be 25 minutes per 455g/1lb plus 25 minutes. Soak the joint in cold water for a couple of hours to remove any excess salt; alternatively, place it in a big saucepan, cover with cold water and slowly bring to the boil, then discard the water.

Cover the bacon with fresh cold water and add the rest of the ingredients for the stock, including the pease pudding. Bring slowly to the boil. Skim the surface when needed and cover with a lid. Calculate the cooking time from this point and reduce to a gentle simmer. Roughly 30 minutes before the end of its cooking time I like to cook my whole vegetables in with the bacon and its broth. When the bacon, pease pudding and vegetables have reached their cooking time, remove them from the saucepan, cut the carrots and celery into quarters and put aside. Remove the rind and excess fat from the bacon.

Remove the pease pudding from the muslin and mash it well with the butter and some black pepper. Use a little of the strained stock as gravy, or as a base for your gravy if you like it thicker. Serve the ham hot with a dollop of the pease pudding, the vegetables, some gravy and some English mustard. Freeze the rest of the stock for soups – it's great for minestrone.

I use minced meat quite a lot at home, usually to make meatballs or burgers. I buy a piece of meat suitable for mincing (ask your butcher and he'll advise you), then either mince it myself or just whack it through the Magimix. The nice thing about mincing your own meat is that you know what is in it, which is reassuring when it comes to cooking it rare, medium or well-done. An alternative is to choose a piece of meat and ask your butcher to mince it for you, in front of you. Don't be put off by the fat on the meat – all kinds of mince, especially sausages, need a good amount of fat to baste the meat naturally during cooking, and most of it cooks out anyway (hence the pool of fat when cooking sausages).

Meatballs

Serves 4–6
900g/2lb meat for mincing or bought minced meat
2 slices of bread
2 level tablespoons dried oregano
½ teaspoon cumin seeds, pounded
½ small dried red chilli, pounded
1 tablespoon finely chopped fresh rosemary
1 egg yolk
salt and freshly ground black pepper
4 tablespoons olive oil
1 tomato sauce recipe (page 237)
2 handfuls of fresh basil, picked and torn
60g/2oz mozzarella cheese, broken up
60g/2oz Parmesan cheese, grated

optional
1 onion, finely chopped
1 clove of garlic
1 tablespoon olive oil
1 level tablespoon Dijon mustard

If your meat is not already minced, whizz it up in a food processor to the required consistency and place it in a bowl. Use the food processor to turn the slices of bread into breadcrumbs. Add the breadcrumbs, dried oregano, cumin, chilli, rosemary and egg yolk to the minced meat and season with 2 level teaspoons of salt and a good twist of black pepper. At this stage you could add your optional ingredients (cooked together gently until tender and allowed to cool). Mix well, and, with wet hands, roll and pat into meatballs the size and shape you want. (These can be cooked straight away or put on greaseproof paper, covered with clingfilm and refrigerated for up to a day.)

Preheat a thick-bottomed casserole to a very hot temperature, add 3–4 tablespoons of olive oil, swirl around the bottom of the pan and add your meatballs. Fry them until they are brown all over, being careful not to break them up but just moving the pan around so that all sides of the meatballs get nicely coloured. Turn the heat down and cover with the tomato sauce (see page 237), loads of ripped up fresh basil and a little broken up mozzarella and grated Parmesan. Cook in the oven at 200°C/400°F/gas 6 for about 15–20 minutes, until the cheese is golden.

VEGETABLES

Slow-cooked Artichokes, Sweet
Cherry Tomatoes, Thyme and Basil

As far as vegetables go, things are moving very fast. Most of our parents were brought up in the post-war years when there was not the vast array of vegetables available that we see nowadays. Consequently a lot of people stick to what they know and, quite frankly, I think that they are missing out big time. Due to the competition between supermarkets and the increasing interest in food of the British public, quality and choice has improved, and will continue to do so. These days the average supermarket gives you the choice of six or seven varieties of tomatoes, five to ten types of mushrooms and vegetables from God-knows-where. Greens and salad leaves are good and are getting better, but are a little bit expensive for my liking. I don't think supermarkets exploit local produce as much as they could, but if they did I know that freshness and quality would improve (though possibly not the price). Things like the Tesco's Finest range, for instance, are a move in the right direction and could be stretched to include vegetables – can you imagine a nice island unit filled with local, organic produce? Fresh beetroots with their leaves, celeriac, asparagus, swede, turnips, special varieties of potatoes, courgettes with flowers, swiss chard, broad beans – the list goes on and on and they all grow so well in England. I know, because my dad grows them.

As a chef, at work, I buy and only accept the best organic vegetables, but at home I can't afford to buy a week's worth of organic veg – they cost a fortune. Hence I compromise, but I suppose you have to find a happy balance. The fact is, organic vegetables do taste better and they're better for you, that's obvious. They don't come in uniform shapes and sizes, and they are generally not cleaned and ready to eat, and I think this is why, in Britain, organic vegetables haven't caught on as much as they should have, especially in this day and age when everyone's busy and running about the place. But for friends, family or special occasions it is worth the effort and money. And by cooking seasonal veg you'll always get a cheaper and better-quality buy.

The only problem I ever see with the average person's home cooking is that vegetables are never seasoned properly. Always season your veg a little at a time, stirring and tasting as you go. By the way, treat yourself to a pack of Maldon sea salt – you might not believe me, but it actually tastes so much better than ordinary salt.

GLOBE ARTICHOKES

Globe artichokes are becoming very popular nowadays. The impression that I get from talking to friends is that they think of them in terms of plain boiled artichokes served with lots of butter, sea salt and freshly ground black pepper. Yes, lovely! But that's just the tip of the iceberg. They can be eaten raw in salads, scattered into pasta dishes at the last minute, deep-fried, baked, braised and grilled.

When you buy globe artichokes make sure that they are not blemished, bruised or bashed about. They should appear 'waxy', as though they have just been cut.

It's probably a good idea if you wear Marigolds for this job, as the artichokes do tend to make your hands go black and they can be very prickly.

Cut the stalks of the artichokes to about 5cm/2 inches from the base of the heart and then cut across the top leaves. One by one, pull the tough outside leaves off. When you have stripped the leaves back to the tender ones, stop and remove the choke with a teaspoon, inserting it into the centre of the flower and carefully turning it. This will remove all the hairy spines. (Once you've done one you'll know exactly how to insert the spoon in the cleanest way, not breaking the sides of the choke.) Now remove the stringy outer skin on the stalk with a peeler. Put the artichokes into water with lemon juice squeezed into it to stop them going brown.

I know this all sounds like a bit of a palaver, but I think it's worth it, and you do get quicker at it; each artichoke should only take about a minute with a bit of practice!

Pan-cooked Artichokes with Lemon, Thyme and Garlic

This is a lovely way to eat artichokes and certainly a good one to try if you are cooking them for the first time.

Serves 4
2 tablespoons olive oil
1 clove of garlic
juice and zest of 1 large unwaxed lemon
8 medium/large globe artichokes, prepared (see page 137)
85ml/3 fl oz dry white wine
salt and freshly ground black pepper
1 good handful of fresh basil, picked, torn or semi-chopped
1 knob of butter

Put the olive oil and garlic into a fairly hot, thick-bottomed, casserole-type pan. Allow to soften but not to colour. Add small strips of lemon zest, which should have no white pith, to the garlic and stir. Then add your quartered or halved artichokes and toss around again with a pinch of salt. (All this time you should be cooking on a semi-gentle heat, just so that your ingredients are sizzling away but not burning or colouring.)

Squeeze in the juice from the lemon and allow it to cook for about 3 minutes, until all the moisture from the pan has evaporated. Add the wine, place a lid on top and allow the artichokes to simmer for about 10 minutes or until tender. Remove from the heat and correct the seasoning. Add the fresh basil and the knob of butter and swirl around. Put the lid back on and allow to sit for 1 minute to let the fragrance of the basil permeate the artichokes. Serve straight away, as an accompaniment for plainly cooked fish or white meats or as an antipasto.

Slow-cooked Artichokes, Sweet Cherry Tomatoes, Thyme and Basil

Serves 4
4 medium/large globe artichokes
olive oil
Maldon sea salt and freshly ground black pepper
2 cloves of garlic, finely sliced
1 handful of fresh thyme leaves
juice of ½ lemon
10 ripe red cherry tomatoes
10 ripe yellow cherry tomatoes
1 handful of fresh basil, torn
1 small dried red chilli, add to taste

Just before you are ready to cook, prepare the artichokes (see page 137) and cut into quarters. Fry gently in a little olive oil in a thick-bottomed pan with a good pinch of salt for about 4–5 minutes with the lid on. Remove the lid and add half the garlic and half the thyme (which can be chopped to intensify the flavour). Allow the garlic to soften. Squeeze in the lemon juice and continue to fry until the moisture has cooked away.

Remove from the heat while you wash and destalk your tomatoes. Put the tomatoes into a bowl with a little olive oil, half the torn basil leaves, a pinch of salt and pepper and the dried chilli. Mix well, then spread evenly in an earthenware-type dish.

Scatter the artichokes and remaining garlic in and among the tomato mixture. Sprinkle over the rest of the thyme and basil. Season with Maldon sea salt and black pepper and drizzle with good olive oil. Place in the oven for about 40 minutes at 180˚C/350˚F/gas 4. If you want to cook it faster you can, but keep an eye on it.

Mashed potato

I love mashed potato. Everyone's made it before, so I'm not trying to teach you a new recipe, but there is good mash and there is bad mash. With no extra effort you can make it really nice and have some simple variations to take a dinner in a completely different direction.

1.4kg/3lb boiling potatoes (Desirée, Maris Piper)
1 tablespoon salt

Wash your potatoes, peel them and wash again. Cut them into equal-sized pieces so they will be ready at the same time. Just cover them with water. Add the salt. Boil until tender (until they fall off the blade easily when stabbed with a knife – or you can just take one out, cut a bit off and taste it). When they are cooked, put them into a colander and allow to sit for 4 minutes, to let all the moisture and water drain and steam off. At this stage you can either place the potatoes back in the pan to be mashed or smashed; or you can use a mouli (one of those things that you spin round and it sort of mashes the potato for you); or you can use a ricer (this is like a big garlic press which pushes the potato through little holes, making it look like rice).

VARIATIONS

Buttered Mashed Potatoes

Add 55–115g/2–4oz butter to your mashed potato. Season to taste with salt and freshly ground black pepper. Add nutmeg to taste and mix.

Creamed Mashed Potatoes

Add 85g/3oz butter and 150ml/5–6fl oz double cream to the mashed potato. Season to taste with salt and freshly ground black pepper. Add nutmeg to taste and mix until smooth and creamy.

Horseradish Mash

Simply add 55g/2oz of butter and 2 heaped tablespoons of horseradish sauce or cream to the mashed potato. If you are lucky enough to get some fresh horseradish, use that – just wash, peel and grate the equivalent of about 1½ tablespoons. Then stir in 2 tablespoons of double cream. Season to taste with salt and freshly ground black pepper.

The fresh horseradish will be a lot more fragrant, slightly hotter and a lot nicer.

Parmesan and Truffle Mash

Add 55g/2oz of butter and 2–3 handfuls of grated Parmesan cheese. Mix this in well and add 1 tablespoon of truffle oil (you can add this to taste).

Truffle oil is now widely sold in supermarkets. It's probably not the real McCoy because the stuff I saw last week was quite cheap, but it is quite an interesting taste anyway and is probably worth trying.

Black Olive Mash

Buy yourself 300g/11oz of the best, or your favourite, black olives and remove the stones. Whizz up about two-thirds of them in a food processor (or very finely chop) and put the remainder in roughly chopped so that you've got some chunks in there as well. Add to the mashed potato. Taste it – it probably won't need any salt because olives are generally quite salty, but give it a little bit of freshly ground black pepper and 1 or 2 tablespoons of good olive oil.

When good English asparagus is in season there is absolutely nothing like it. Simply cooked, boiled, steamed, grilled or roasted, it can be served alone as a starter or as a vegetable and served with cooked meat or fish. When buying asparagus I always look for fat, plump, deep green asparagus but the thin ones can be just as gorgeous. Always avoid slightly white and woody stalks and budding tips. The quickest way to check the quality of your asparagus is hold it at either end and slowly bend and snap it – it should snap naturally where the stalk is edibly tender. If you are lucky it will still leave you with a fair-sized piece.

I don't believe in mucking around too much with asparagus – whatever flavours you add should be subtle, such as good olive oil or butter, or extremely complementary, such as anchovy butter or Gorgonzola.

Boiled Asparagus with Any Interesting Melting Cheese

When I'm on my way home from work I just pick up any interesting cheese that will melt and be sticky and stringy and coat my beautiful asparagus. It's dead easy and it makes perfect sense.

Serves 4
680–900g/1½–2lb fresh asparagus, trimmed
   and peeled if necessary
115–140g/4–5oz interesting melting cheese
   (Gorgonzola, taleggio, Parmesan are good)
1 small handful of fresh herbs, to include basil,
   marjoram and parsley
salt and freshly ground black pepper

Cook your asparagus in boiling, salted water until tender. Drain and place in a bowl with your broken up cheese, herbs and seasoning. Toss over until the cheese has semi-melted and serve.

Steamed Asparagus with Lemon and Anchovy Butter

This is a perfect combo – you can't season asparagus while you're steaming it, so the slight saltiness of the anchovies seasons it for you when you toss it in the butter. Check out flavoured butters (see page 227).

Serves 4
55g/2oz anchovies, the best you can find
140g/5oz butter
small pinch of dried chilli
freshly ground black pepper
juice of 1 lemon
680–900g/1½–2lb fresh asparagus, trimmed and peeled if necessary

Whizz up the anchovies in a food processor (or chop them finely), and add the butter, chilli and pepper. Add the lemon juice, to taste. Steam the asparagus in a fast-boiling steamer (or in a colander over a pot) until tender – taste one. You can toss your anchovy butter and asparagus together before serving, or simply serve the steamed asparagus with a knob of anchovy butter on the top.

Grilled Asparagus with Olive Oil and Sea Salt

Serves 4
680–900g/1½–2lb fresh asparagus, trimmed and peeled if necessary
4 tablespoons extra virgin olive oil (or butter)
Maldon sea salt

For this recipe I use one of those grill pans that you just chuck on the hob or gas and allow to get smoking hot. Sling your asparagus on and allow to char on both sides. By the time it's evenly charred it should be perfectly cooked. Serve drizzled with the best olive oil you can get (or with butter), and season to taste with Maldon sea salt.

Roasted Asparagus with Cherry Tomatoes, Black Olives and Basil

I think this recipe is choice. The sweetness of the tomatoes, the smokiness of good black olives, the fragrance of fresh basil and the freshness of your asparagus make an orgasmic combo.

Serves 4
680–900g/1½–2lb fresh asparagus, trimmed and peeled if necessary
1 good handful of black olives
20 cherry tomatoes, small, sweet and ripe
3 tablespoons olive oil
1 clove of garlic, finely sliced
1 good handful of fresh basil
salt and freshly ground black pepper
small pinch of dried red chilli, crumbled

Mix all the ingredients together in a bowl and then place in a hot pan or roasting tray. Cook in a preheated oven at 225°C/425°F/gas 7 for about 10–12 minutes, turning 2 or 3 times. Serve.

I like to cook the asparagus a little longer than usual for this dish – not so that it is overcooked and mushy, but so it holds its shape while getting a chance to suck up all the lovely flavours in the tray around it.

Braised Cabbage with Smoked Bacon and Peas

This can take boring old cabbage in a completely different direction. It is good served with whole roasted birds (game or chicken), fresh spring peas and smoky bacon. Using a mixture of cabbages makes the texture, colour and taste more interesting.

Serves 8

1 savoy cabbage, plus equivalent amount of spring greens,
   brussel tops or cavalo nero, very roughly chopped
2 tablespoons olive oil
6 rashers dry-smoked streaky bacon, cut across
   into 1cm/⅜in strips
1 dessertspoon chopped rosemary
1½ cloves of garlic, finely chopped
140ml/¼ pint chicken or vegetable stock or water
170–200g/6–7oz fresh, podded peas
salt and freshly ground black pepper
85g/3oz butter

Strip back the outer leaves of your cabbage until you reach the tender leaves. If these outer leaves are not wilted, yellow or have not been eaten by caterpillars, remove the tough stem and wash them thoroughly (these are normally the greenest leaves, which are better for you – they taste and look better but need a touch longer to cook). Roughly chop and place in a bowl and put to one side.

Remove most of the tough stalk from the tender inside of the cabbage and roughly chop the leaves. Add the olive oil to a hot thick-bottomed pan and begin to fry off the bacon. After 1 minute add the rosemary and garlic and mix to combine the flavours – the smell will be fantastic. At this point the garlic should soften and just begin to take on colour and the bacon should be going golden. Add your green outside cabbage leaves and a little bit of your stock or water, stir, place a lid on the pan and steam for 1 minute. Then add the rest of your cabbage and greens, the podded peas and a pinch of salt and pepper. Stir in the rest of your stock.

Replace the lid and simmer for 12–15 minutes, until the cabbages are still bright in colour but tender enough to eat. Turn the heat off, add the butter and leave for about 5 minutes. Season before serving.

Stir-fried Chinese Greens with Ginger, Oyster and Soy Sauce

For this dish I use any mixture of good Chinese greens I can get my hands on. It's tasty and very quick to make.

Serves 4–6
300–400g/11–14oz mixed Chinese greens – pak choy,
   bok choy, Chinese broccoli (gai larn), baby spinach
3 tablespoons walnut oil
1 tablespoon sesame oil
½ tablespoon thinly sliced ginger
4 spring onions
2 tablespoons oyster sauce
1 tablespoon soy sauce
2 pinches of sugar
juice of 1 lime
salt and freshly ground black pepper

Remove any blemished outside stalks from the greens. Put the spinach to one side so that you can add it to the wok or pan at the last minute, as it cooks very quickly. Prepare the rest of the Chinese greens; I normally cut the Chinese broccoli into strips and the pak and bok choy into quarters. Plunge the greens into boiling water for about 1½ minutes until just tender, and drain well.

Put the oil and the ginger into a very large, hot wok or other suitable pan and cook for about 30 seconds. Add the finely shredded spring onions and the rest of the ingredients apart from the seasoning. Stir, then add the spinach and toss so that everything is coated in sauce. The vegetables will sizzle and stir-fry. The oyster and soy sauce will reduce, just coating the greens. At this point season to taste. Stir-fry for a further minute and serve immediately.

Spicy Roasted Squash

Serves 6
1 medium/large butternut or onion squash (1–1½kg/2–3lb)
2 teaspoons coriander seeds
2 teaspoons dried oregano
½ teaspoon fennel seeds
2 small dried red chillies (or to taste)
1 teaspoon salt
1 teaspoon freshly ground black pepper
1 clove of garlic
1 tablespoon olive oil

Wash the squash, then cut it in half with a large sharp knife (cut off one side and roll the squash on to the cut edge to make this safer and easier). With a large spoon, remove the seeds from the squash (try roasting these with a little touch of oil and some sea salt and have them with drinks, like peanuts – they're really nice). Cut the squash lengthways into quarters and then cut the quarters in half – you should have approximately 2.5cm/1 inch thick, boat-shaped wedges of squash. Put them into a bowl.

Put all the dried herbs and spices into a pestle and mortar and pound them up with the salt and pepper to make a fine powder. Once you've done this, add the garlic clove and pound it into the spices. Scrape out the contents into the bowl and add 1 tablespoon of olive oil. Toss the squash thoroughly in this herb and spice mixture, making sure that all the pieces are well coated.

Place the squash pieces in a line, skin side down, on a baking tray. Roast them in the oven at 200°C/400°F/gas 6 for about 30 minutes, or until tender. The spicy flavour will cook into the squash, and the squash will crisp slightly, the skin becoming caramelized and chewy.

I use this particular vegetable for so many different things: as a base for a filling in a ravioli, for bread, for risotto and as a vegetable to accompany any roast. When I first showed it to my mum she didn't like the idea of it, but she actually loved the taste with the spices. We eat it quite a lot at home now. Do try it – it's really nice, cheap and accessible.

Roasted Red Onion with Thyme and Butter

Serves 6

Try to get 6 equal-sized medium to large red onions. Remove the first layer of skin. With a knife, just take the bottom of the core end of the onion off, to give it a flat base, and make 2 cuts in a cross-shape in the top, cutting half way down (do not cut right through into quarters). Push some chopped or pounded fresh thyme into these gaps with a good pinch of salt (it's important to get the salt right into the gaps) and a little knob of butter. I prefer to cook the onions in an earthenware dish on a thin layer of sea salt or I put them in with my roast chicken or lamb and they cook quite happily in the same tray. Place in the oven at 200°C/400°F/gas 6 for 30–35 minutes.

These onions are great with a roast, so tasty and sweet.

Vegetable Tempura

Tempura batter is very handy and easy to make. You can use it with just about any vegetable, as long as they're cut thin enough so that the vegetable can just cook and soften in the same time as it takes for the batter to crisp. Good tempura should be crispy and is one of those things that should be made and cooked quickly and eaten straight away. These can be eaten alone as a starter with a good sprinkle of rock salt, halves of lemon or lime and possibly some of the dips. The battered vegetables also make a nice side dish, especially good with simply cooked meat or fish and a salad.

200g/7oz plain flour
100g/3½oz cornflour
ice-cold water (preferably soda or sparkling)
selection of vegetables (see below)

Add all the flour to a bowl. With the handle of a spoon, or a chopstick, mix and stir in the ice-cold water until the mixture is slightly thicker than double cream consistency. Make a point of not mixing thoroughly, as tempura is renowned for lumps of flour.

Dip your chopped vegetables (courgettes, onions, aubergines, carrots, sweet potatoes, fine green beans, broccoli, wild mushrooms, fresh herbs, pak choy and bok choy – any vegetables will work but these are the most commonly used) into the batter mixture and shake off any excess.

Deep fry your vegetables at 200°C in a deep fat fryer (you can use a wok or a frying-pan if you don't have anything else – you just need about 7cm/3 inches of clean oil) until the batter is light golden in colour and crisp. (Any large amounts of hot oil in a kitchen, especially in woks which are not always that sturdy, scare the shit out of me – please be careful and don't leave the pan unattended.) Turn the vegetables at intervals to ensure that both sides are cooked equally and then fish them out with a slotted spoon, shaking off any excess oil. Place them on kitchen paper and eat as soon as possible. The reason that I keep going on about eating them so quickly is because as your hot cooked vegetables cool down inside the batter they begin to steam, making the batter less crisp as time goes on.

PULSES

In this country, at the moment, we're all getting much more interested in dried beans and rice. They're really nutritious, dead cheap, and the choice and quality are definitely getting better. I think the improvement in quality has a lot to do with us becoming less tolerant of all the second-class stuff that we used to accept so readily from other countries.

The idea of drying beans goes back thousands of years. It was done to pre-serve foodstocks, so that people could carry on eating the local produce well after the season had finished, and quite honestly nothing has really changed today. The only criteria for the best produce is that it is grown on good soil, picked at its best and dried as soon as possible. Pulses shouldn't be dirty, have stones in or look tatty. A sign of age in dried beans is when they start to shrivel and crack. Most pulses keep well for up to a year; after that they become harder to reconstitute and tend to burst or crack when cooked.

At the River Café, as soon as the quality of the fresh beans starts to go (towards the end of the season) then it is straight on to that year's dried beans. (Rose and Ruth always get samples from different suppliers to com-pare the cooked quality.) In my opinion good-quality dried beans are almost as good as fresh ones. There are so many things you can do with pulses: put them in salads, stews, soups, casseroles, or simply use them as you would a vegetable.

How to cook pulses

I think we should have a little chat about what we're going to do with these pulses. What you have to get into the habit of doing is, before you go to bed, just chucking a mugful of washed pulses into cold water to soak overnight. This will shorten the cooking time next day and help to prevent them from splitting during cooking. Borlotti, cannellini, black-eyed and butter beans, chickpeas and split peas all have to be soaked in this way. Pick out any dodgy-looking ones. I don't soak lentils because they don't take that long to cook.

The cooking times tend to vary for pulses. There's no great mystery about the cooking time, it all really depends on their age and how long they have been soaking. As a rough guide, after an overnight soak, rinse, bring them to the boil in fresh water and simmer for about 1 hour, or until tender (just taste one). You can pop a peeled potato and a scored tomato in with the pulses, as this helps to soften the skin, and you can also put in some herbs or a bou-quet garni to infuse some flavour. I sometimes put in a rasher of smoked bacon, which I take out and discard after the pulses are cooked.

Borlotti Beans with Olive Oil and Lemon Juice

Borlotti beans go well with lamb and they're great in stews, risottos and soups. This is a really simple recipe that you can serve hot as an accompaniment to any roast, or cold, tossed in a bowl with some fresh rocket as an interesting salad or perhaps beside some nice cured meats such as parma ham or prosciutto.

Serves 6
340g/12oz borlotti beans, soaked overnight
2 cloves of garlic, peeled
1 plum tomato
a small bunch of fresh sage
olive oil and lemon juice dressing (see page 42)
salt and freshly ground black pepper

Rinse the soaked beans and add the garlic, tomato and sage. Cover with cold water. Bring to the boil, place the lid on and gently simmer for 1–1½ hours or until tender. Drain, discard the tomato, sage and garlic and dress generously while warm with the olive oil and lemon juice dressing. Check the seasoning, and serve hot or cold.

Marinated Chickpeas with Chilli, Lemon and Parsley

The chillies really make this dish, don't be afraid of them. They won't blow your brains out because, when deseeded, they just give a really fresh, fragrant flavour with a little bit of warmth. Trust me!

Serves 6
1 handful of fresh parsley, with the stalks separated
  from the leaves and the leaves roughly chopped
340g/12oz chickpeas, soaked overnight
1 large peeled potato
2 cloves of garlic, peeled
olive oil and lemon juice dressing (see page 42)
2 medium or 4 small fresh chillies, halved, deseeded
  and finely chopped

Tie the parsley stalks together. Rinse the soaked beans, add the stalks, whole potato and garlic, and cover with water. Bring to the boil, place the lid on and simmer gently for 1½ hours or until tender, skimming as necessary. Once they are cooked discard the stalks, potato and garlic. Drain and, while still hot, dress with the olive oil and lemon juice dressing, the chillies and the chopped parsley leaves.

This is lovely served at room temperature with grilled fish or tossed into a salad. And I like it semi-smashed and smeared over some toasted bread.

Humous

I like humous just as a dip, with roasted lamb, and I especially like having it at my local 'Kebab Kid' in pitta bread sandwiched between a crisp salad and a lamb Shewama, extra large! Mind you, I'm normally a bit 'bevvied' by then and probably anything tastes nice, as you probably all know! But seriously, everyone likes humous, it's great with lamb and very easy to make.

Serves 4
340g/12oz chickpeas, soaked overnight
1 small dried red chilli
½ teaspoon cumin seeds or ground cumin
salt and freshly ground black pepper
1 clove of garlic, peeled
1½ tablespoons tahini (sesame seed paste –
*   sold in most supermarkets)*
4 tablespoons extra virgin olive oil
lemon juice to taste (approx. 2 tablespoons)

Rinse the soaked chickpeas. Cover with water and cook for 1½ hours or until tender, skimming as necessary. Drain, saving a little of the cooking water.

In a pestle and mortar pound the chilli and cumin with a teaspoon of salt. In a food processor, finely chop the garlic, then add the chickpeas, chilli, cumin and tahini and pulse them until smooth. Add the salt, pepper, oil and lemon juice to taste. If you prefer the humous a bit thinner, add a little of the cooking water until you're happy. And there you have it!

Pease Pudding

This is my version of the old-fashioned pease pudding. It goes great with hot boiled bacon and English mustard. It is really nice if you simmer all the ingredients, in a piece of muslin, in with the bacon from the beginning (see page 131).

Serves 6
340g/12oz yellow split peas, soaked overnight
1 small potato, peeled
1 small onion or shallot
1 clove of garlic, peeled
1 small bunch of herbs (rosemary, sage, thyme, bay)
2 cloves
30g/1oz butter
salt and freshly ground black pepper

Rinse the soaked peas, add the potato, onion, garlic, herbs and cloves, and cover with cold water. Bring to the boil, put the lid on, and simmer slowly for about 1½ hours, until tender. Drain, remove the herbs and the cloves, then add the butter, salt and pepper and mash well. Serve hot.

Puy Lentils Braised with Rosemary and Garlic

For this recipe you can either stew the lentils on the hob or braise them in the oven. I prefer to braise them, so you'll need a pan with a tight-fitting lid that can go in the oven as well as on the hob. They have such an edge on plain boiled lentils and are excellent served with roasted pigeon or grilled venison.

Serves 6
55g/2oz pancetta or smoked streaky bacon
340g/12oz Puy lentils
1 tablespoon olive oil
3 heaped tablespoons chopped fresh rosemary
1 red onion or 2 shallots, finely chopped
2 cloves of garlic, finely chopped
850ml/1½ pints chicken stock
2 tablespoons extra virgin olive oil
½ tablespoon red wine vinegar
salt and freshly ground black pepper

Slice the pancetta or bacon across into fat matchsticks. Give the lentils a quick wash. Using a thick-bottomed pan, heat 1 tablespoon of olive oil and add the pancetta. Fry until it is slightly coloured and then add the rosemary, onion and garlic. Cook for a further 2 minutes, then add the lentils and fry for about 1 minute. Add the stock, put the lid on, bring to the boil and simmer in the oven for 1 hour at 160°C/310°F/gas 2½ or until tender, stirring occasionally. By this time a lot of the stock will have been absorbed. Add 2 tablespoons of your best extra virgin olive oil, ½ tablespoon of red wine vinegar, and black pepper and salt to taste (bear in mind that the pancetta is a bit salty). Serve hot.

Black-eyed Beans with Spinach and Balsamic Vinegar

You can serve this hot, on its own, as a vegetable, or at room temperature as a salad or an antipasto. My favourite way of serving it is with some juicy roast pork (see page 109).

Serves 4
340g/12oz black-eyed beans, soaked overnight
2 cloves of garlic, chopped
1 tablespoon unsalted butter
1½ tablespoons extra virgin olive oil
255g/9oz fresh spinach, roughly chopped
salt and freshly ground black pepper
1 tablespoon balsamic vinegar

Rinse the soaked beans, and cover with water, bring to the boil and simmer for about 1 hour or until tender. Drain. Fry the garlic in the butter and oil until golden (this takes just seconds). Add the drained black-eyed beans and the roughly chopped spinach and fry until the spinach has wilted (about 1 minute). Season and add the balsamic vinegar.

Butter Beans with Marinated Tomato, Chilli and Basil

Try this one on its own with a green salad, or served warm with roasted white fish such as cod or monkfish. It goes really well with chicken and pork as well.

Serves 4
340g/12oz butter beans, soaked overnight
11 medium/large ripe plum tomatoes
1 large bunch of basil, roughly chopped
2 medium/large fresh red chillies, deseeded and finely chopped
1–1½ tablespoons red wine vinegar
3 tablespoons extra virgin olive oil
salt and freshly ground black pepper

Rinse the soaked beans and cover with water. Add 1 tomato (the acid in the tomato makes the skins less tough). Bring to the boil, cover the pan and simmer for about 1½ hours or until tender.

Remove the cores from the remaining 10 tomatoes and score a cross on top of each. Place into boiling water and remove fairly quickly, or when you can peel the skin off. Take out the seeds, roughly chop the tomatoes, place in a bowl and add the remaining ingredients.

Drain the cooked butter beans (discarding the tomato cooked with them) and gently stir them into the tomato marinade. Leave for about 15 minutes, as this will improve the flavour. Serve warm or cold.

Baked Butter Beans with Leeks, Parmesan and Cream

I like to have this as a side dish with a roast. It's absolutely superb! And nice with pan-fried lamb chops and some spinach.

Serves 4
340g/12oz butter beans, soaked overnight
1 tomato (optional)
3 medium leeks
2 large cloves of garlic, chopped
1 knob of butter
1 tablespoon oil
salt and freshly ground black pepper to taste
140ml/¼ pint cream
1 good handful of freshly grated Parmesan cheese

Rinse the soaked beans and cover with water. Add the tomato (the acid in the tomato makes the skin less tough). Cover with water, bring to the boil, cover the pan and then simmer for about 1½ hours or until tender. Drain (discarding the tomato).

Slice the leeks as thinly as possible, across and at an angle. Fry them with the garlic in the butter and oil, and add a pinch of salt and pepper to taste. Stir in the butter beans and add the cream. Place in a shallow dish, sprinkle with the Parmesan and bake in a hot oven (230°C/450°F/gas 8) for 10–15 minutes until golden.

Cannellini Beans with Herb Vinegar

When I think of cannellini beans, I think of a big bowl of lovely thick Italian soup with ripped up crusty bread and green peppery virgin olive oil on top. (See page 19.)

Serves 4
340g/12oz cannellini beans, soaked overnight
2 tablespoons white wine vinegar
4 tablespoons extra virgin olive oil
fresh herbs
salt and freshly ground black pepper to taste

Rinse the soaked beans and cover with water. Bring to the boil and simmer for about 1 hour or until tender. Toss gently with the rest of the ingredients. Serve warm or cold.

RISOTTO AND COUSCOUS

If I asked most people if they made risotto at home I reckon most would say 'no', and would think it was just poncy restaurant food. Well, I suppose they're right in the way that most good restaurants include risotto on their menus somewhere these days. But risottos are really meant to be cooked at home – you can prepare them easily, and can make them warming and whole-some or delicate and light. They are cheap and can be eaten all year round. I think a few restaurants bastardize the whole method and principle of risotto. The perfect risotto should slowly ooze across the plate, not be made into a tower or a mould – the fact that it isn't moving tells you that it's too dry. Yuck!

Okay, so you've got this pack of risotto with this fat plump rice and it's just crying out for things to complement it. You can use almost anything to flavour it: fragrant root vegetables, herbs, fish, meat, mushrooms, offal, shellfish, cheese, wine . . . anything really. Just remember that the rice itself is nutty and moreish so the flavour added can be quite delicate. You need to strike a good balance between the rice and the flavour. The rice should be cooked until just soft but should still retain a good bite. The sauce sur-rounding and binding the risotto will be a mixture of subtle stock, thickened slightly with the starch gently oozing out of the rice (I know I keep saying 'ooze', but it is actually quite an oozing sort of thing, risotto).

Anyway, what I am going to do now is give you a really solid, decent risotto base method and then give you five of my favourite variations. I reckon once you've tried one you'll be surprised yourself how easy it is. And if you don't feel too confident, remember this isn't restaurant food, it's peasant food!

Just a few points to remember

- For good and consistent results buy Arborio or Carnaroli risotto rice.
- Don't wash the rice, as you want it to retain all the starch.
- Try to acquire a sturdy, thick-bottomed pan, preferably as high as it is wide. The thick bottom allows for a nice equal heat and the high sides will help to prevent the moisture from evaporating too quickly.
- Get yourself some good stock – obviously homemade is best (see pages 223–6), but if you don't have time you can buy ready-made stock.
- Always try to use fresh Parmesan (preferably Parmigiano Reggiano) from a chunk rather than ready-grated. It tastes completely different and it's always better if you grate it just before you use it. It should be used almost as an extra seasoning that rounds off all the flavours. It's used in most risottos, apart from seafood ones.

Basic Risotto Recipe

If you follow this recipe, I promise you'll be making some of the best risottos out. The real secret of a good risotto, I'm afraid, is that you have to stand over it and give it your loving and undivided attention for about 17 minutes, but it's worth it. The recipe is in stages; I am going to give you five of my favourite risottos – all variants of this basic recipe.

Serves 6
approx. 1 litre/2 pints stock (chicken, fish or vegetable as
   appropriate – see pages 223–5)
1 tablespoon olive oil
3 finely chopped shallots or 2 medium onions
½ a head of celery, finely chopped (discard any tough outer sticks)
Maldon sea salt and black pepper
2 cloves of garlic, finely chopped
400g/14oz risotto rice
100ml/3¾fl oz dry white vermouth (dry Martini or Noilly Prat)
   or dry white wine
70g/2½oz butter
85–100g/3–3½oz freshly grated Parmesan cheese

Stage 1. Heat the stock. Then in a separate pan heat the olive oil, add the shallot or onion, celery and a pinch of salt, and sweat the vegetables for about 3 minutes. Add the garlic and after another 2 minutes, when the vegetables have softened, add the rice. Turn up the heat now. At this crucial point you can't leave the pan, and anyway, this is the best bit.

While slowly stirring, continuously, you are beginning to fry the rice. You don't want any colour at any point (so remember, you're in control, and if the temperature seems too high, turn it down a bit). You must keep the rice moving. After 2 or 3 minutes it will begin to look translucent as it absorbs all the flavours of your base (it may crackle at this point, that's fine). Add the vermouth or wine, keeping on stirring as it hits the pan – it will smell fantastic! It will sizzle around the rice, evaporating any harsh alcohol flavours and leaving the rice with a tasty essence.

I must admit I'm a sucker for dry vermouth. When it cooks into the rice it seems to give it a really full but subtle flavour and leaves a wicked sweetness that works perfectly with the rice. White wine is lovely, probably more delicate and fresh. Try both – see what you think.

Stage 2. Once the vermouth or wine seems to have cooked into the rice, add your first ladle of hot stock and a pinch of salt (add small amounts of salt to taste while you are adding the stock). Turn down the heat to a highish simmer (the reason we don't want to boil the hell out of it is because, if we do, the outside of the rice will be cooked and fluffy and the inside will be raw). Keep adding ladlefuls of stock, stirring and allowing each ladleful to be absorbed before adding the next. This will take about 15 minutes. Taste the rice – is it cooked? Carry on adding stock until the rice is soft but with a slight *bite*. Check seasoning.

Stage 3. Remove from the heat and add the butter and the Parmesan, saving a little of the latter to go on top if you like. Stir gently. Eat it as soon as possible while it retains its moist texture.

Serve it on its own or with a crisp green salad and a hunk of crusty bread. Beautiful.

Borlotti Bean, Pancetta and Rosemary Risotto

This is my favourite risotto of all time – it is absolutely superb. The pancetta and rosemary is a marriage made in heaven and the borlotti beans look and taste great and make a real change in a risotto.

   This risotto is excellent with any leftover rabbit or hare, which can be broken up and added at the last minute.

Serves 6
basic risotto recipe (see page 170), using chicken or vegetable stock
55g/2oz pancetta or smoked, streaky bacon, sliced thinly crosswise
2 tablespoons finely chopped fresh rosemary
255g/9oz cooked borlotti beans

Follow the basic risotto recipe. Fry the sliced streaked bacon until golden and slightly crisp and add it at Stage 1 with the rosemary. At Stage 3 add the warm, cooked borlotti beans.

Mushroom Risotto with Garlic, Thyme and Parsley

The nice thing about mushroom risotto is that you can use just one or a mixture of your favourite mushrooms. The supermarkets now have such a good selection of fresh mushrooms: field, oysters, shitake, chestnut, pieds de mouton, girolles, chanterelles and blewits. I try not to wash mushrooms, as they soak up the water (which you don't want) and the mushrooms end up being boiled. Just gently brush off any dirt or dust with a pastry brush or a tea-towel. You can make a good risotto with dried mushrooms; dried porcini are very good and reconstitute easily.

Serves 6
basic risotto recipe (see page 170), using chicken or vegetable stock
255g/9oz mushrooms (one type, or a mixture)
3 tablespoons olive oil
1 small handful of thyme, picked and chopped
1 clove of garlic, finely chopped
salt and freshly ground black pepper
1 handful of parsley, roughly chopped
1 pinch of chilli powder
a squeeze of lemon juice

Slice the mushrooms thinly, but tear the girolles, chanterelles and blewits in half. Don't cook all the mushrooms at once – do them in 2 or 3 batches. In a very hot pan heat a tablespoon of olive oil and add the mushrooms and thyme. Cook for about 1 minute, toss them, then add the garlic and a pinch of salt. (It is important with mushrooms to season them slightly as they cook.) Cook for another couple of minutes and then taste – if they are nicely cooked add some parsley, a very small pinch of chilli powder and a squeeze of lemon juice. Toss again, taste again – by now they should be pretty much perfect. Chop half the cooked mushrooms.

At basic recipe Stage 2, after the first ladle of stock has been added, add the chopped mushrooms, and add the remainder at Stage 3.

Spicy Squash Risotto with Thyme and Mascarpone

Serves 6
basic risotto recipe (see page 170), using chicken or vegetable stock
spicy roasted squash (see page 148)
2 heaped tablespoons fresh thyme leaves
2 heaped tablespoons mascarpone

First of all roast your squash. Divide it in half. Remove the skin from one half and roughly chop the flesh. With the other half, leaving the skin on, chop slightly finer. At Stage 1 add the thyme. At Stage 2 add the batch of squash which has had the skin removed. At Stage 3 add the rest of the squash (the batch with skin on) and the mascarpone.

Minted Asparagus and Pea Risotto

This is a great summer risotto. When buying asparagus, always choose small ones – the bigger ones are often tougher and stringier. The tips shouldn't have any flowers or be budding. When I buy fresh peas I always open them up in the shop and taste one. They should be very sweet (even when raw), with thin delicate skins – not like little bullets. Lovely!

Serves 6
basic risotto recipe (see page 170), using chicken or vegetable stock
455g/1lb asparagus
340g/12oz fresh peas
1 handful of fresh mint, picked
1 handful of grated Parmesan cheese

Trim your asparagus from below the tips to the base (I use an old-style potato peeler). Remove the bottom of the stalk and discard. Take off the tips and blanch in salted water until just tender, then finely chop the rest of the stalks and put to one side. Blanch the peas until just tender in *unsalted* water (this is important, because salt toughens the skin). Finely chop the mint.

At the end of Stage 1 add the roughly chopped asparagus stalks and half the peas. At Stage 3, add the blanched tips of asparagus, the rest of the peas and the mint. Mint should always be added to taste as it can vary in strength and flavour. Serve with a good sprinkling of Parmesan over the top.

Seafood Risotto with Fennel and Chilli

Here's a recipe that can be used for any kind of seafood. You can buy your seafood at any stage of its preparation. A live crab or lobster is such a treat, and you can't get any fresher than that, but good-quality prepared seafood will work with this recipe too. For this risotto I replace half the butter with olive oil – and remember, you don't need Parmesan.

Serves 6
basic risotto recipe (see page 170), using fish stock
400g/14oz seafood (one type or a mix)
1 large fennel bulb, very finely chopped (reserve the green tops)
2 medium red chillies, deseeded and chopped
6 anchovy fillets (even if you don't like these you must add them
  as they will give the risotto a certain depth of flavour – though
  you won't taste them)

First prepare your seafood (see page 178). At Stage 1 add the chopped fennel and chillies. Just before you add the rice, add the anchovies and let them melt (about 30 seconds). At Stage 3, just before removing from the heat, add the seafood (to warm it, *not* to cook it). Serve sprinkled with the reserved chopped fennel tops.

Marinade for lobster, crab and prawns

2 tablespoons olive oil
juice of 2 lemons, to taste
1 handful of fresh basil, chopped
1 handful of fresh parsley, chopped
salt and freshly ground black pepper

(To cook and prepare lobster, see page 105.) Mix the marinade ingredients, and check seasoning.

Add lobster and crabmeat directly to the marinade. Uncooked prawns should be gently sautéd in a little olive oil and butter first, and the shells removed.

To prepare mussels and clams

olive oil
½ clove of garlic
a little white wine

Wash the mussels, remove the beards and discard any that are already open. Get a pan really hot and add the oil, then the garlic, then the mussels or clams and enough white wine to cover the bottom of the pan. Cover with a tight-fitting lid and steam for 3–4 minutes, shaking the pan until the mussels have opened. Remove the meat and discard the shells. Strain the cooking liquor and save to use as part of the stock.

To prepare white fish

olive oil
fennel seeds, crushed
pinch of chilli powder
salt and freshly ground black pepper

Use any nice flaking fish such as hake, mullet, cod or bream. Roast or pan-fry the fish with some olive oil and sprinkle with crushed fennel seeds, chilli powder, salt and freshly ground black pepper.

Couscous is so tasty, quick to make, cheap and versatile that I can't understand why it isn't more widely used in this country. I can only assume that people don't know enough about it. It comes from North Africa. It is a cereal processed from semolina and dried and rolled into little pellets; it's been around for hundreds of years. You can use it as you would rice – to mop up sauces, or as a salad, or perhaps more classically with a spicy Moroccan-style lamb stew.

When you use couscous you are actually reconstituting it, so to serve it hot you treat it in much the same way as steamed or boiled rice. Either pour boiling water or stock on it and allow to stand for about 10 minutes, or steam it in a pan with a close-fitting lid for 5 minutes. If you are using it as a salad, it should be mixed raw with the dressing and a little cold water so that, after about 15 minutes, the flavours and fragrance of the dressing will be absorbed into it (this is how I really like it).

Steamed Couscous Infused with Caraway and Fennel Seeds

This couscous is light and fluffy and should be served steaming hot. It's good with lamb or chicken stew.

Serves 4
425ml/¾ pint stock or water
1 level tablespoon fennel seeds
1 level tablespoon caraway seeds
salt and freshly ground black pepper
250g/9oz couscous
butter

Bring the stock or water to the boil with the caraway and fennel seeds and season with salt and pepper. Pour this over the couscous, stir, and leave to stand for 15 minutes. Place in an oven dish lightly rubbed with butter, and cover with lightly buttered tinfoil. Place in an oven at a low heat (150°C/300°F/gas 2) for about 10–15 minutes – this will gently steam the couscous.

Spicy Couscous

Spicy couscous is lovely with grilled or roasted lamb, a little gravy and a little dollop of mint sauce or salsa verde (see pages 231, 233). This may look complicated but it takes only 20 minutes to cook and is really easy.

Serves 4
425ml/¾ pint stock or water
1 medium shallot or onion, finely chopped
1 tablespoon olive oil
2 knobs of butter
1 level teaspoon cumin seeds
1 heaped teaspoon coriander seeds
1 heaped teaspoon fennel seeds
½ small dried chilli, or to taste
1 teaspoon salt
1 bay leaf
1 clove of garlic, finely chopped
1 tablespoon red wine vinegar
1 teaspoon sugar
255g/9oz couscous

Bring the stock to the boil. In a thick-bottomed, deepish pan slowly fry the shallot or onion with the olive oil and half the butter, without colouring. In a pestle and mortar smash up the cumin, coriander, fennel, chilli and salt. (If you haven't got a pestle and mortar you can do this by spreading out a tea-towel, putting your spices in the middle, folding the tea-towel up and smashing it with a rolling-pin or hammer. This works quite well but be careful not to break anything!) Add the spices, bay leaf and garlic to the onions and continue to fry – they should look and feel like marmalade, but not be coloured or burnt. Add the vinegar and sugar and reduce to a syrup. Add the couscous and stir. Add the hot stock and simmer for 15–20 minutes, stirring occasionally. Fork through the rest of the butter to lighten.

Couscous Salad

Uncooked but marinated in a salad dressing, couscous has a little more bite and texture than when boiled or steamed. Serve this as a main course salad, or with pitta bread and grilled chicken. It keeps well in the fridge until the next day or so. The herbs are very important but you can really do your own thing with the other ingredients – experiment!

Serves 4
255g/9oz couscous
olive oil and lemon juice dressing (see page 42)
285ml/½ pint cold water
2 red peppers
2 small shallots or 1 red onion, finely chopped
¼ clove garlic, finely chopped
1 medium fresh chilli, deseeded and chopped
2 tomatoes, deseeded and diced
juice of 1 lemon
1 teaspoon red wine vinegar
2 handfuls of fresh herbs (basil, coriander or flat-leaf parsley)
1 tablespoon olive oil
salt and freshly ground black pepper

Put the couscous in a bowl and toss with the olive oil and lemon juice dressing. Add the water, stir, and leave to stand for 15 minutes or so for the dressing to be absorbed. Meanwhile, grill the peppers whole, turning at intervals, until blackened all over. Place in a bowl (still hot), cover with clingfilm and leave to steam, then peel, deseed and chop finely. (This might sound like a bit of a fuss, but you can do it while the couscous marinates.)

Put the peppers in a bowl and add the shallots, garlic, chilli, tomatoes, lemon juice, vinegar and herbs. Drizzle with olive oil, season to taste, and stir. Leave for 15 minutes then incorporate with the couscous.

BREAD

Twister Bread, Ciabatta, Cottage Bread

It's amazing how many chefs I know have never made a loaf of bread. For me it was the start of something I could never stop doing. If you go to a friend's home or to a restaurant for dinner and there is homemade bread it really adds something extra. If it's done really well, that's just pukka. I first made bread properly in a château in France. I learnt loads and had great respect for the *boulanger*, but it also seemed very clinical and exact – not for the wrong reasons, it just seemed a bit dull.

It wasn't until I met Gennaro Contaldo, from the Neal Street Restaurant in Covent Garden, that I was humorously introduced to the world of bread. *Big bread, flat bread, long bread, thin bread, rolled bread, filled bread, loadsa blooming bread* – it was easy and it tasted wonderful. Because I was so keen to learn, I used to work long hours at the restaurant. I'd get up at 3 a.m., drive traffic-free into Covent Garden, and there for four and a half hours I would make bread with Gennaro, at first shadowing him, then helping him. Nothing was exact, but by following simple rules and using good ingredients (and a little bit of soul), his bread was consistently superb.

We would make a huge batch of basic dough, split it, and derive from it about eight different breads. The nice thing was that, as Gennaro taught me, he never implied that his ways were carved in stone. He always made sure that recipes were left open for innovation, which was very generous of him, as most good chefs think that their methods are the only ones. Not Gennaro. His encouragement has kept me thinking ever since.

I consider bread-making to be an art, but it requires a little knack in getting used to touching and kneading the dough. That sounds very clichéd but it's true. The first time I started working Gennaro's dough it stuck all over me. It was everywhere. Gennaro laughed and suggested that I treat the dough like a woman, delicately and gently but using a degree of strength and vigour. This improved my bread-making skills a treat, as well as my sex life! Superb! This experience stayed with me and is the basis of all my bread-making. Basically, as long as you want to make good bread and you enjoy it you're half-way there!

Basic Bread Recipe

Homemade bread is easy to make, impressive and versatile. It doesn't matter if you make it regularly or only for special occasions, it's your bread and it has its own character. Once you've made one of these breads I know you'll try more, and then you'll really have cracked it!

This is such a good recipe. One basic set of ingredients, split up into stages so that you can use any of the variations at the correct stage.

30g/1oz fresh yeast or 21g/¾oz dried yeast (3 × 7g sachets)
30g/1oz honey (or sugar)
625ml/just over 1 pint tepid water
500g/just over 1lb strong flour
500g/just over 1lb semolina flour (if you can't get hold of any
*   semolina flour then plain flour will do)*
30g/1oz salt
some extra flour and semolina for dusting

Stage 1. Dissolve the yeast and honey (or sugar) in half the tepid water.
Stage 2. On your largest available clean surface (even a big bowl will do if surfaces are limited), make a pile of the flour, semolina flour and salt. With one hand, make a well in the centre. (If possible, it is preferable to warm the flour and semolina flour.)
Stage 3. Pour all the dissolved yeast mixture into the centre and with four fingers of one hand make circular movements, from the centre working outwards, slowly bringing in the dry ingredients until all the yeast mixture is soaked up. Then pour the other half of the tepid water into the centre and gradually incorporate all the flour to make a moist dough. (Certain flours may need a little more water, so don't be afraid to adjust the quantities.)
Stage 4. Kneading! This is the best bit, just rolling, pushing and folding the dough over and over for 5 minutes. This develops the structure of the dough and the gluten. If any of the dough sticks to your hands, just rub them together with a little extra flour.

You can do Stages 2, 3 and 4 in a food mixer if you like, using the dough hook attachment.

Stage 5. Flour both your hands now, and lightly flour the top of the dough. Make it into a roundish shape and place on a baking tray. Score the dough with a knife – this allows it to relax and prove more quickly.

Stage 6. Leave the bread to prove for the first time. Basically we want it to double in size. This is probably the best time to preheat the oven (see oven temperatures for each bread variation). You want a warm, moist, draught-free place for the quickest prove, for example near the cooker, in the airing cupboard, in the plate warmer of a cooker or just in a warm room, and you can cover it with clingfilm if you want to speed it up. This proving process matures the flour flavour and should take approximately 40 minutes to an hour and a half, depending on the conditions.

Let's just talk about proving so you know what's going on. The yeast is now feeding on the honey or sugar in the warmth of the tepid water. In theory the three things that all bacteria need to grow are heat, moisture and food. Any excess of these three things will kill the yeast (as well as salt, which we have used to season the bread – it's not half so nice without it, but it does slow down the proving to some extent).

Stage 7. Right, it's double the size and time to knock it back. Knead and punch the dough, knocking all the air out of it, for about a minute.

Stage 8. Shape the dough into whatever shape you want – round, flat, filled, or whatever (see the variations to follow) – and leave to prove a second time in a warm place until the dough is double its size.

The important thing is not to lose your confidence now; if you don't think it's proved enough, leave it a bit longer and check the warmth or for any draughts.

Stage 9. Now it's time to cook your loaf. After all your hard work, don't spoil your efforts. You want to keep the air inside the loaf, so don't knock it, put it very gently into the oven and don't slam the door. Bake according to the recipe time and temperature given in the variations which follow, or until it's cooked. You can tell if it's cooked by tapping its bottom (if it's in a tin you'll have to take it out) – if it sounds hollow it's cooked, if it doesn't then pop it back in for a little longer.

Stage 10. Place the bread on a rack to cool – for cooking time see each recipe variation. You're going to love this bread!

Focaccia

For 2 large or 4 smaller focaccia

This is my favourite Italian flatbread. It is not very difficult to make. Follow the basic recipe until Stage 8, then split the dough into half or quarters. Roll or push it out to an oval shape roughly 1½cm/½ inch thick; don't fuss around for perfection, it's supposed to be rough and rustic, so what a great excuse for a beginner! Place on a baking tray liberally dusted with semolina, and smear evenly with one of the toppings shown below. Finally, make those characteristic holes by pushing all your fingers deep into the dough many times, which allows the flavour of the topping to penetrate. After about 45 minutes it will prove to that classic 3cm/1¼ inches high.

At basic recipe Stage 9, bake for about 15 minutes at your oven's highest temperature until ready. As soon as the focaccia comes out of the oven, feed it with a good drizzle of your very best olive oil and a light scattering of sea salt. You can eat the focaccia as soon as it has slightly cooled.

TOPPINGS

Below are some toppings that I like, but it's real fun to do your own thing. Toppings mustn't be too heavy, just a light scattering of interesting flavours. Try marinated sun-dried tomatoes, black or green olives, mixed herbs, herb oils, some interesting cheeses (not too much, though; the Italians would probably use up any old dry cheese for this).

The following amounts are for the whole quantity of bread but you may well wish to, say, make 4 different toppings for 4 small focaccias, in which case just divide the amount accordingly.

Basil and Olive Oil Topping

This is the easiest topping and very tasty. Finely chop 1 clove of garlic and a good bunch of basil. Add roughly three times as much oil as you have of the basil mixture, a squeeze of lemon juice, salt, freshly ground black pepper and sometimes a crushed dried chilli – gives nice warmth! Be subtle.

Wash about 15 new potatoes and slice as thinly as possible. Put in salty (or minty) boiling water for 2 minutes. Drain the spuds, place in a bowl, and coat with a generous amount of your best olive oil. Season with salt and freshly ground black pepper, add 1 finely chopped clove of garlic and a handful of chopped fresh rosemary. Smear and push the mixture all over the bread. This is really nice if you flick some rosemary on top before baking, for a really rustic look.

I'm a real fried onion boy myself! This topping is tasty, light and fragrant. Peel and halve, from the core to the top, 3 average size red onions (or about 6 shallots), then slice as thinly as you can. Heat a frying-pan with a good lug of oil. Add 1 finely sliced clove of garlic, a good handful of thyme leaves, and then add the onions or shallots. Add a pinch of salt and fry fast, keeping it on the move, for 4 minutes (the idea is to cook fast and caramelize the onions, but not to over-colour or burn them). Next, add about 3 tablespoons of red wine vinegar and simmer for a further 4 minutes. Add some salt and freshly ground black pepper and a little extra virgin olive oil, smear everything over your bread, then throw some thyme leaves over it. Looks great!

Beer Bread

Beer Bread

For 1 large loaf

At Stage 1 you exchange the water for your favourite beer and follow the method until Stage 8. Make 6 equal-sized balls and place them next to each other in a greased round cake tin (5 round the edge and one in the middle). Sprinkle with either a light dusting of flour or some caraway seeds. Then prove until doubled in size (the balls will prove into each other). At Stage 9 bake at 225°C/425°F/gas 7 for 20–25 minutes or until done. Allow to cool for at least 45 minutes.

This bread doesn't have a really strong taste of beer – just the mellow, malty undertones coming through.

Twister Bread

I like this bread made with purple pesto, but green pesto is fine. (The recipe for pesto is on page 232.) Follow the basic dough recipe. At Stage 8, divide the dough into 2 equal parts. Roll or push out each piece of the dough into a squarish sheet 1cm/½ inch high and 30cm/12 inches long. Smear pesto generously over the sheet of dough and roll up like a swiss roll. Then with a really sharp knife cut across into 4cm/1½ inch slices. Place the slices close together on a greased baking tray, cut side upward (rather like Chelsea buns). At Stage 9 bake at 225°C/425°F/gas 7 for 15–20 minutes. Allow to cool for 30 minutes before eating.

Cottage Bread

For 2 loaves

Follow the basic recipe until Stage 8, then split the dough into 2 equal parts. Make a rough ball out of each part and fold the bottom sides into the bottom centre, which should improve the shape. Place the loaves on a baking tray liberally dusted with semolina, then gently press down on the top of the loaves to flatten them slightly. Sprinkle generously with flour, and then with a sharp knife score 4 lines on the top. Prove for about 45 minutes to an hour.

At basic recipe Stage 9, bake for 20–25 minutes at 225°C/425°F/gas 7. When ready, leave for at least an hour before eating.

Snap Bread

This bread is great for using up leftover bits of dough, so you don't need to make the full basic recipe quantity unless you want loads of them. But they do keep in an airtight container for a couple of weeks and freeze really well.

After basic recipe Stage 7, roll your dough to a thin sheet, about 1cm/½ inch high and 30cm/12 inches long. Flour the top of the bread liberally and use a large knife or a pizza cutter to slice 1cm/½ inch strands. Place these on a baking tray sprinkled liberally with semolina. Prove for ½ an hour. At Stage 9, bake for about 10 minutes at 200°C/400°F/gas 6 (you want to dry them out so that they stay crispy). This bread is wicked if friends come round for a drink and you serve some humous, guacamole, black olive dips, salsas, relishes and all that sort of thing.

Ciabatta

For 3 ciabattas

Follow the basic recipe, adding around 6 tablespoons of olive oil at Stage 8. Then split the dough into 3 equal parts. Using both hands, roll each portion into a 25cm/10 inch sausage shape, then, using the heel of your hand, press every inch all the way along the bread to widen and flatten it. The shape at this stage should be roughly 30cm/12 inches long, 2½cm/1 inch high and 10cm/4 inches wide. Place the dough on a baking tray liberally dusted with semolina. Dust the dough with flour and score about 5 times, at an angle.

Prove for about 45 minutes and, at basic recipe Stage 9, bake for about 25 minutes at 225°C/425°F/gas 7 until ready. Allow to cool for about ½ an hour before eating it.

Snap Bread

Rolls

For about 12 medium rolls

Before you start to make these rolls, here are some suggestions to tickle your fancy, some quite easy, some easier. But I'd love to think that you might experiment with your own ideas for flavours. Don't forget to get your flavours sorted *before* you start to make the dough.

Follow the basic recipe until Stage 4, then split the dough into sections, one for each different type of roll you want. Immediately scrunch your chosen flavour well into the dough (all flavours should be at a warm room temperature), then allow to prove. This will take about 40 minutes. When double the size, knock back as at Stage 7. At Stage 8, bearing in mind that these will double in size, make into the shapes and sizes you want (either a round or a fat cigar shape would be good). Place on a baking tray liberally dusted with semolina, lightly flour the top of the rolls and score them with a sharp knife. At Stage 9 bake at 225°C/425°F/gas 7. Check the rolls after 10 minutes – the cooking time will vary according to the size of the rolls. Place the rolls on a rack and leave for at least 15 minutes before eating.

Plain or Simply Scented Rolls

The fact is a plain roll is lovely – you don't have to do anything apart from shape it, prove it and bake it. However, you can scent the dough with some chopped fresh herbs such as thyme, rosemary, oregano, summer or winter savory, marjoram, basil or chives, or some pounded spices such as coriander seeds, caraway seeds, chillies, celery seeds, mustard seeds or fennel seeds. You can use them singly, or make a marriage of two. The last thing I want to do is to give you weights or amounts; this should be to your own taste.

Personally I am more generous with the herbs than with the spices, as I think the latter should be more subtle.

Roasted Hazelnut and Apricot Rolls

These rolls need roughly equal quantities of hazelnuts and dried apricots (the moister apricots are better for this purpose). You should aim for a total amount of nuts and apricots roughly the equivalent of a quarter of the weight of the dough used, but the amount can happily vary in either direction.

Quite simply, roast your hazelnuts in the oven with a drizzle of olive oil and a pinch of salt until golden (this does not take long and it's dead easy to burn them). It's nice to crush or chop half the hazelnuts finely, to get the flavour in there, and crack the other half for texture and looks. The same idea applies to the dried apricots when you are chopping them.

Spiced Squash Rolls

Don't turn your nose up at the thought of this one (like my mum did!) It's a really interesting flavour. I first made this bread when I had some leftover spicy roast pumpkin. I chopped it up and whacked it into the dough, and I was well chuffed with the results. It was a great addition to a summer lunch, served still warm with a hunk of runny Brie, a pile of salad and a beer. For this recipe you will need a quantity of the squash from the recipe on page 148 – again, aim for an amount of squash roughly equivalent to a quarter of the weight of the dough to be used.

Pizzas

For 4 pizzas

I make pizzas all the time at home; I like to do them fairly thin because I think that way you get a better balance of topping and base. (I always eat one and freeze the other three, half cooked for 5 minutes with no topping – it makes it so easy when you come home from work late.) Personally I don't like a mouthful of dough like you get with American pizzas; it should be quite crisp and delicate. I'm giving you my favourite toppings (each enough for 1 pizza) but obviously you'll all have your own favourites.

First prepare your chosen topping (see the suggestions below). Follow the basic recipe until Stage 8, then divide the dough into 4 equal pieces. Roll each portion into a ball, lightly flour the work surface and roll (or push) it out (always rolling away from you and turning 45° after every roll). Roll to roughly ¾cm/⅜ inch high (to prove to about 1cm/½ inch high), bearing in mind pizzas do not have to be perfectly round. Place on a sheet of lightly greased kitchen foil or a baking tray and add the toppings. It is not necessary to prove thin pizzas as you do bread, so 10 minutes proving should do the trick, and they will continue to expand in the oven. At Stage 9 bake for about 10 minutes at 240°C/475°F/gas 9, until the dough looks crisp and golden and the toppings look cooked. Eat as soon as possible.

If you are using a pizza base you have frozen, you need not thaw it. Add your topping to the frozen base, and cook for an extra 5 minutes at 225°C/425°F/gas 7.

MY FAVOURITE TOPPINGS

Tomato, Basil and Mozzarella Topping

Lightly smear the pizza base with tomato sauce (see page 237). Roughly scatter with a generous handful of whole or torn basil leaves. Break up some mozzarella and scatter the pieces evenly(ish) round the pizza. Add some freshly ground black pepper. Cook for about 10 minutes at 240°C/475°F/gas 9. When ready, drizzle with your best olive oil.

I usually use a pestle and mortar for this but you can get the same effect by chopping finely. Smash up a handful of washed thyme and a good pinch of salt. When it looks like a coarse paste, add ½ a clove of garlic and smash that into a paste too. Add a squeeze of lemon juice and about 2 tablespoons of your best olive oil. Now prepare the artichokes: 1 or 2 artichokes per pizza will be plenty, and you can either use fresh ones (see page 137) or the prepared ones available in jars. With a sharp knife slice them first in half, then as thinly as possible lengthwise. Immediately toss them gently in the thyme mixture to prevent discoloration, then evenly smear the pizza with the mixture. At the last minute I sometimes mix a handful of rocket in with it. Bake in the oven for 10 minutes at 240°C/475°F/gas 9, then roughly shave some nice long bits of Parmesan over the top (I use a potato peeler at home).

This is a quick topping. Wash 3 plum tomatoes (I don't take the skin off but if you want to, simply score, place in boiling water for 15 seconds, then peel). Slice in half, scoop out the pips and core, and roughly chop. Place them in a bowl and season with salt (not too much, remember the pancetta is quite salty), freshly ground black pepper and 1 small, fresh, finely sliced chilli (you can use a fried chilli but be careful because they're hot). Add ¼ of a clove of garlic, finely chopped, ½ a handful of whole fresh oregano leaves and ½ a handful of chopped fresh oregano. Add a couple of drips of red wine vinegar. Toss the mixture and smear over the pizza (do this fairly quickly, as the salt will draw the water out of the tomatoes and the mix must not be too watery). Pancetta is available from most delis or good supermarkets, but if you can't get it, use dry smoked streaky bacon. Lay about 6 strips of really thinly sliced pancetta across the pizza. Cook for 10 minutes at 240°C/475°F/gas 9.

Turrón Nougat Semi-freddo

Desserts are funny old things. When it comes to making them, a lot of people won't touch them with a bargepole, they just buy frozen or prepared stuff (ummm!). Other people just have a very small repertoire of maybe two or three desserts that they do very well, and by varying their fillings or flavours increase their repertoire to about a dozen different desserts. Now that's the spirit we want!

When you go out to a restaurant, and are paying a lot of money, you expect something a bit special. As a chef I see loads of desserts which are far too fussy for the home situation – I just know that no one will want to make them.

I believe the answer is to give you some simple recipes that you can personalize, but without the fussy stuff. So here are some nice and easy basic recipes which can be the platform for your own inspiration. I want you to wander around the markets and shops and, when you see something that catches your eye, something juicy-looking or sweet-smelling and irresistible, take it home and make something lovely from these recipes with it.

Baked Fruit

Don't underestimate the simplicity of fresh, ripe fruit in season. Try it baked – it takes on quite a different character. The warm, tart flavours of the fruit with the sweet vanilla sugar are really interesting and taste quite different from fruit eaten raw.

Buy some good-quality plums, apricots, nectarines, peaches, pears, cherries, figs, strawberries. The quantities are entirely up to you; bake as little or as much as you want. Wash the fruit, and halve, stone or core if necessary. You could add some lovely pink sticks of rhubarb, washed and sliced, or peel and slice some bananas. Place the fruit in a shallow heatproof earthenware-type serving dish, add a couple of drips of brandy if you like, and sprinkle with vanilla sugar (basically sweeten to your taste, but if the fruit is naturally quite sweet then obviously use less sugar than if the fruit is very sour and tart). Preferably grill them or roast them in the oven at the highest temperature – not too long, just long enough to soften them slightly but still keep their shape (it should take roughly 4 minutes, although rhubarb will take a couple of minutes more). Serve with some whipped vanilla cream, crème fraîche, vanilla ice-cream or mascarpone sweetened with vanilla sugar. Classy!

Vanilla Sugar

Don't buy vanilla essence and don't buy ready-made vanilla sugar. It's so expensive, you don't get much and you can so easily make a much better version yourself. You should use vanilla pods. Although the pods are quite expensive, the recipe works out much cheaper in the long run because of the amount you can make.

Don't buy vanilla pods that are dry and hard – buy them fat, sticky and squashy. What we want to do is infuse the natural flavour of the vanilla pods into the sugar. It is perfectly fine, and obviously quicker, just to pop the pods in an airtight container with the sugar; you will achieve a more subtle flavour. I really like this recipe, though, because you get the maximum flavour from the pods.

1kg/2lb caster sugar
4 vanilla pods

You need a food processor for this one. Put your vanilla pods in the mixer, blitz, scrape the sides and blitz again. Add all the sugar and blitz for about 2 minutes. Sieve the mixture into a bowl, return any lumps to the food processor and blitz again. (You may want to repeat this process if you want it really fine.) The result will be a slightly ashy-coloured mixture – now that's real vanilla sugar!

Store it in an airtight container. It should last you for ages.

Mascarpone Cream

Now this is a 'naughty but nice' cream. It is great on the side with baked fruit, but also useful as a filling for those last-minute fruit tarts. Just fill a pastry case with it, cover with fruit, give it a quick glaze if you like (1 tablespoon jam and 1 tablespoon water warmed in a pan) and Bob's your uncle and Fanny's your aunt.

1 tablespoon vanilla sugar (see page 200)
255g/9oz mascarpone cheese

Simply mix the sugar into the mascarpone.

Vanilla Cream

This cream has a lighter texture than mascarpone cream. It goes well with almost any dessert.

255ml/9fl oz double cream
1 tablespoon vanilla sugar (see page 200)

Whip the cream and sugar until the mixture stays in soft peaks. Don't over-whip.

Semi-freddo

I don't know anyone who hasn't groaned with pleasure at eating this! It is so delicious and really quick and easy to make. This recipe, with variations, is a great substitute for ice-cream because, although I personally love making ice-cream, who does make it at home in reality? Almost no one! We just go and buy some. I know I do.

Semi-freddo is special in its own right – it's as diverse and refreshing as ice-cream. I have given you some of my favourite variations, but you can experiment with the basic recipe yourselves.

For best results, it's important to gather all your ingredients together and make it as quickly as possible (no pressure intended! It's just better to freeze it with as much air in as possible). After preparing your flavouring, the semi-freddo takes literally 4 minutes to make. Once made, pour it into any chosen container – I like to use a large earthenware dish. Then place it in the freezer.

I always make this quantity. If you make more than you need, just scoop the leftover piece into serving portions and put it back into the freezer. Then, when you want a piece, take it out of the freezer, let it thaw slightly in the fridge to 'semi-freddo' (semi-frozen), and remember – the same rules apply to this as they do to ice-cream, in that you can't leave it hanging about and then re-freeze it. That's asking for trouble!

Semi-freddo is quite rich. To complement it perfectly, serve it with some fresh fruit beside it – raspberries, strawberries, blueberries, cherries – whatever's in season. In Italy they often serve it with caramel or toffee, and even a fruit coulis sometimes. I don't really like all that stuff, but it's up to you. Just don't try too hard.

Serves 12
1 vanilla pod
55g/2oz sugar
4 large fresh free-range eggs, separated
500ml/17fl oz double cream
salt

Remove the seeds from the vanilla pod by scoring down the length and scraping the seeds out of each half. (Don't throw the empty pod away, pop it in with some sugar – see page 200.) Whisk the vanilla seeds and sugar with the egg yolks in a large bowl until pale. In a second bowl whisk the cream until soft peaks form. (Important! Please don't over-whip it.) Then in a third bowl whisk the egg whites with a pinch of salt until they form very firm peaks (this is when you can pull the egg whites in any direction and they will stay like it). At this point add the flavouring you have chosen (see the variations to follow, or choose one of your own), the cream and egg whites, to the egg yolk mixture. Gently fold in. Immediately scoop the contents into your chosen container. Cover with clingfilm and freeze until you're ready to eat it.

This is one of my real favourites, roasted hazelnuts in caramel, just superb! To make caramel successfully, it needs your undivided attention for about 10 minutes. You can't leave it for a moment, and do be careful with kids around – caramel burns are some of the worst kind, no joke! I've never burnt myself on caramel and nor should you, just use your head and resist the temptation to taste it at any time.

310g/11oz peeled hazelnuts
200g/7oz sugar
4 tablespoons water

Roast the hazelnuts in the oven at 225°C/425°F/gas 7 until golden (about 4 minutes). Really watch them, because if you over-roast them they go bitter and you can't use them. Put the sugar and water in a thick-bottomed pan and place on a medium to high heat. The mixture will start to bubble and then turn into a clear syrup. To begin with, it will gradually start to colour in parts or from the sides. Gently and carefully shake the pan, just moving it to mix the patches of colour. When it's all golden brown, carefully tip it away from you and gently add the nuts. Turn the heat down to a simmer and gently stir to coat the nuts in caramel. When the caramel is dark golden brown, turn it out on to a clean, lightly oiled tray, or on to greaseproof paper on a surface that won't burn. It will cool to a flattish solid sheet.

When completely cooled (which takes about 20 minutes), smash it up roughly and pulse it in the food processor until the pieces are still quite chunky (very approximate size about ½cm/¼ inch). Remove about half the praline, then pulse the rest to a powder (or put it in a tea-towel and bash with a rolling-pin), and add both lots of praline to the semi-freddo mixture.

Figs and Honey Semi-freddo

310g/11oz dried figs, chopped
3 large tablespoons honey, or to taste
6 fresh figs

Remove the little hard stalks from the dried figs. Pulse them in the food processor with the honey till just chopped. Wash the fresh figs, remove the stalks, and roughly chop. Mix everything together. Add to the semi-freddo mixture.

Turrón Nougat Semi-freddo

The French make nougat, the Italians make turrone and the Spanish make turrón. They are very similar, come in a variety of flavours and combinations and usually include nuts, candied fruit, honey, coffee and chocolate. Some are chewy, others are crunchy; crunchy is best for this recipe.

400g/14oz turrón nougat (flavour of your choice
  and the best one that you can find)
150g/5oz unsalted pistachio nuts
55g/2oz chocolate (70% cocoa solids)
2 large tablespoons honey

Smash the nougat up roughly and pulse it in the processor until the pieces are fine (or put it in a tea-towel and bash it with a rolling-pin). Then add the pistachio nuts, holding some back to sprinkle on top afterwards. Add the nougat to the semi-freddo mixture. Grate the chocolate on top and drizzle with honey.

Everybody loves steamed puddings. I know I do, they always make me think of the ones my mum makes to have after the Sunday roast. I love them with lots of custard!

I'm going to give you a superb spottier dick pudding followed by the basic steamed pudding recipe with some pukka variations. These are really easy to make and always go down well, no matter who you are entertaining. Great with custard, mascarpone or vanilla cream (see page 201). You must serve your pudding whole at the table, steaming hot and drizzled with your topping. It's the only way to serve it.

A Spottier Dick Pudding

This is a proper 'blokes' pudding – loads of custard, a little warmed syrup over the top and even some cream. Superb!

Serves 6
115g/4oz suet
455g/1lb mixture of sultanas, raisins and currants
zest of 1 lemon or 1 orange
115g/4oz plain flour
115g/4oz sugar
115g/4oz breadcrumbs
1 level teaspoon ground ginger (or to taste)
¼ nutmeg, grated
pinch of salt
1 egg
140ml/¼ pint milk

Grease a 1½ litre/3 pint pudding basin. Mix all the ingredients together, except the egg and milk. Add the beaten egg and milk and mix well. (I do this in a mixer but you can do it by hand, no problem.) Put the mixture in the basin, cover with tinfoil or a cloth, and put the basin in a pan with water half-way up the sides of the basin. Bring the water to the boil, put on a tight-fitting lid, and simmer for 3 hours, remembering to top up with boiling water now and then.

Basic Steamed Pudding Recipe

225g/8oz self-raising flour
pinch of salt
85g/3oz caster sugar
115g/4oz shredded suet or butter
1 large egg
8 tablespoons milk

Grease a 1 litre/2 pint pudding basin. Spoon in your chosen flavour (see the variations below). Mix together (in a mixer or by hand) the flour, salt, sugar and suet or softened butter. Then add the egg and milk and mix well. Put into the pudding basin, covered with greaseproof paper or a cloth tied with string or tinfoil, and stand the basin in a pan with water half-way up the sides of the basin. Cover with a tight-fitting lid. Bring to the boil, then simmer for about 2 hours, topping up with boiling water if necessary. Don't let it boil dry and make sure it does not go off the boil.

VARIATIONS

Chocolate, Orange and Nut Pudding

Follow the recipe for chocolate pudding above, adding 120g/4oz finely chopped nuts (walnuts, almonds or hazelnuts) and the zest of an orange to the basic pudding mix.

Jam Pudding

Simply spoon 3 large tablespoons of jam into the bottom of the pudding basin.

Chocolate Pudding

basic steamed pudding recipe (see page 208),
  adding 3 tablespoons cocoa to the flour

Chocolate sauce
115g/4oz icing sugar
115g/4oz good-quality chocolate
115g/4oz butter, softened
2 tablespoons milk

Put a little water in a saucepan and on it place a bowl. Bring the water to the boil and then turn down to a simmer. Put the sugar and chocolate in the bowl and stir until melted. Remove from the heat, stirring in the butter. Then add the milk and stir it in. Finally pour a quarter of the mix into the bottom of the prepared pudding basin, saving the rest which can be reheated and drizzled over the whole steaming pudding when serving. Looks great!

Ginger Pudding

basic steamed pudding recipe (see page 208)
1 tablespoon ground ginger
55g/2oz stem ginger, chopped

Add the ground and chopped ginger to the basic pudding recipe.
    This is nice with some golden syrup. Either put the syrup at the bottom of the pudding basin at the beginning, or warm and pour it over the top at the end.

Syrup Pudding

Simply spoon 3 large tablespoons of golden syrup into the bottom of the pudding basin.

Fruit Crumble

This just has to be the quickest dessert to make in the whole world! Everyone loves it, and you can use whatever fruit is in season. Serve it with custard, cream, ice-cream, mascarpone or vanilla cream (see page 201).

There are several different variations on the theme. I'll give you the basic recipe to start with.

Serves 6
Crumble
225g/8oz plain flour
115g/4oz butter
90g/3oz sugar
pinch of salt

Fruit
455g/1lb fruit, washed and prepared
3 tablespoons sugar

Just stick all the crumble ingredients in a food processor and blitz until it resembles fine breadcrumbs (you can also do this in a mixer or by hand – just rub the mixture between your hands).

Put the fruit into a shallow ovenproof serving dish and sprinkle with the sugar. Spread the crumble mix over the prepared fruit. Give the dish a bit of a shake and bake it in the oven at about 200°C/400°F/gas 6 for about half an hour or until the top is evenly golden. (If it starts to go darker round the edge, turn the oven down a little.)

You can replace half the flour with porridge oats or replace some of the flour with chopped or ground nuts. You can even add a teaspoon of ground ginger.

Any fruit or combination of fruits works for this recipe: apples, apples and blackberries, apricots, rhubarb, blackcurrants, gooseberries, peaches, plums, raspberries, pears, summer fruits (a great crumble warm, with ice-cream!). I can't think of anything that you can't use. Try using soft brown sugar instead of white – it seems to make a more caramelly juice. How about some orange segments or chopped stem ginger in with the rhubarb, or some toasted almonds in with the peaches or apricots? Apple crumble is always nice with some lemon zest and juice, or perhaps a few sultanas. Try some fresh figs with honey instead of the sugar. I bet you have loads of your own ideas – try them. It's such an adaptable recipe.

NB I don't add any water to the fruit because it makes its own juice, but you can add a couple of spoonfuls if you like. Also I never cook the fruit before making the crumble; there's no need.

As this is a book about what I cook and what I find easy at home I'm not going to hide the pastry recipe in a small corner in the back of the book. I find it such a simple thing to make, pre-make, freeze and vary; it is such an asset to home cooking and so versatile.

Short Crust Sweet Pastry

To make 2 × 30cm/12 inch tart moulds
250g/9oz butter
200g/7oz icing sugar
a medium pinch of salt
500g/just over 1lb flour
4 egg yolks
4 tablespoons cold milk/water

Making the dough

You can make this pastry by hand or in a food processor. Cream together the butter, sugar and salt and then rub or pulse in the flour and egg yolks. When this mixture has come together, looking like coarse breadcrumbs, add the cold milk or water. Pat and gently work together to form a ball of dough. Lightly flour and push, pat and squeeze into shape. The idea is to get your ingredients to a dough form with the minimum amount of movement, i.e. keeping your pastry flaky and short (the more you work it the more elastic it will get, causing it to shrink in the oven and be chewy – ooooh no, matron).

Allowing to rest

I normally roll the pastry into a really large, short and fat sausage-shape, wrap it in cling-film and place it in the fridge to rest for at least *1 hour*.

Lining the mould

Carefully slice off thin slivers of your pastry (don't try to slice frozen pastry) lengthways, around 5mm/⅛ thick. (I personally like it around that thickness as it's delicate, but you can make it thicker if you want, it just takes longer to cook. Place the slivers in and around the bottom and sides of your tart

mould, just fitting them together like a sort of jigsaw. Then simply push the pieces together, level out, then tidy up the sides by pushing with your thumb and either cleaning off the excess pastry from the rim of the mould, or allowing it to hang over the edge – which is quite rough but I like it. Once you've finished lining your tart mould you must again allow it to rest for at least an hour, preferably in a freezer (I always store my pastry in the freezer because it keeps so well). I always line two tart moulds and freeze one for another day (or you could make more if you want, just double the recipe, as it takes no extra time). It's so easy to grab a tart out of the freezer, bake it in minutes and fill it with something simple or elaborate, and if guests turn up or you just want to make a nice dessert, it makes pudding a piece of cake!

Baking the tart

To start with I always bake tart shells for around 15 minutes at 180°C/ 350°F/gas 4 which will cook the tart all the way through, colouring it slightly. Once completely cooled it can be filled with any of the uncooked fillings, such as *Fruit-filled Mascarpone Tarts* and *Chocolate Tart* (see page 221) which will hopefully provide a basis for you to make up and vary your own.

With baked fillings such as *Almond Tart* or *Lemon and Lime Cream Tart* you'll have to bake the tart blind first, which means cooking the shell at 180°C/350°F/gas 4 but only for about 12 minutes, so that it's only lightly coloured but just cooked through. Another way, commonly used, is to fill the tart shell with clingfilm or greaseproof paper and fill it with beans (you can use rice, lentils, peas, whatever), the idea being that you pack the beans in so tightly that they will stop the sides of the pastry from dropping. Cook for 10 minutes and then carefully remove the beans and cook for a further 5–10 minutes. Yes, this is a bit of a performance and I only ever do it when I'm having bad luck, quite honestly if you take your tart shell straight out of the freezer and place it in a preheated oven you shouldn't have any problems.

After baking blind, you add your filling and bake further until the filling is cooked (see recipes for cooking times).

Almond Tart

1 tart case, baked blind (see page 214)
400g/14oz blanched whole almonds
350g/12oz unsalted butter
300g/11oz sugar
3 whole free-range eggs

In a food processor, blitz the whole almonds to a fine powder and put into a bowl. Then blitz the butter and sugar until light and creamy. Add this to the almonds with the lightly beaten eggs and fold in until completely mixed. Place in the fridge to firm up slightly. Once it has chilled, fill the tart case – not too generously or it will spill over, and not too meanly unless you are going to add some fruit.

If making a fruit and almond tart it is always a good idea to pick fruit that is slightly unripe – when it is cooked it will contrast with the sweetness of the almond filling. My favourites are fat cherries, nectarines, peaches and pears. Just push the fruit into the almond mixture once you've filled the tart case.

Bake on a tray at 180°C/350°F/gas 4 for approximately 1 hour, until the almond mix has become firm and golden. Allow to cool for about ½ an hour and serve with ice-cream, crème fraîche or vanilla cream (see page 201).

This tart will keep for 2 days, but it's quite handy to freeze the raw almond mix and the blind-baked tart shell for any surprising and presumptuous friends.

Lemon and Lime Cream Tart

This tart's one of my favourite combinations – lemon and lime to me is so much more refreshing than just plain old lemon. If you want to bring out the fragrance of the lime even more, simply grate the zest of 4 limes and add to the filling mix at the beginning. This filling isn't made from a curd recipe, it's gently baked in the oven after you have baked the pastry shell blind, so you are left with a really soft and silky filling and a short and crisp pastry shell.

1 tart shell, baked blind (see page 214)
340g/12oz caster sugar
8 large free-range eggs
350ml/12fl oz double cream
200ml/7½fl oz lime juice
100ml/3¾fl oz lemon juice

With this particular tart, as it has a moist filling, it's important to egg-wash the uncooked tart shell before adding the filling. This adds a sort of water-proof layer and keeps the pastry crisp and short for longer.

Bake your tart shell blind (see page 214). Whisk together the sugar and eggs in a bowl. When they are well mixed, slowly stir in the cream and the juices. Put the cooked tart shell back into the oven and then pour the filling into it – I find this reduces spillage. Bake for around 40–45 minutes at 180°C/350°F/gas 4 or until the filling is set but still semi-wobbly in the middle (obviously different ovens will cook at a different rate so it is good for you to try this tart a couple of times to gauge exactly when you should take it out of the oven). After cooling for an hour, the semi-wobbly filling will have firmed up to the perfect consistency; soft and smooth. If you cut it before it has had time to rest it will pour out or be extremely gooey.

You can dust it with a little icing sugar, if you wish. Serve with a huge pile of fresh raspberries or strawberries. Whatever you decide to serve it with should be quite simple so that you let the tart do the talking.

Baked Chocolate Tart

I think this tart is best served with some seasonal soft fruit (blueberries, raspberries, strawberries).

1 × 25cm/10 inch flan or tart shell, baked blind (see page 214)
140g/5oz butter, unsalted
150g/5½oz best-quality cooking chocolate (70% cocoa solids)
8 tablespoons cocoa powder, sifted
small pinch of salt
4 eggs
200g/7oz caster sugar
3 tablespoons golden syrup
3 medium heaped tablespoons sour cream or crème fraîche

Place the butter, chocolate, cocoa powder and salt in a bowl over a pan of simmering water and allow to melt slowly, stirring occasionally until well mixed in. In a separate bowl beat the eggs and sugar together until light and well creamed, and then add the golden syrup and sour cream or crème fraîche. Stir your chocolate mixture into this mixture, scraping all the chocolate out with a spatula. Once you've mixed it well pour it into the pastry shell. Place into a preheated oven for 40–45 minutes at 150°C/300°F/gas 2. During cooking a beautiful crust will form on top.

Carefully remove the tart from the oven and allow to cool on a rack for at least 45 minutes, during which time the skin will crack and the filling will shrink slightly.

Simple Chocolate Tart

Simple Chocolate Tart

This chocolate tart is great for those chocofreaks who turn up out of the blue as it is dead quick to make. I think this particular tart cries out for a slightly thicker pastry shell. The better the chocolate you can buy, the tastier it will be.

1 tart shell, baked blind (see page 213)
315ml/11fl oz double cream
2 level tablespoons caster sugar
the smallest pinch of salt
115g/4oz butter, softened
455g/1lb best-quality cooking chocolate, broken up
100ml/3¾fl oz milk
cocoa powder for dusting

Place the double cream, sugar and pinch of salt in a pan and bring to the boil. As soon as the mixture has boiled, remove from the heat and add the butter and chocolate. Stir until it has completely melted. Allow the mixture to cool slightly, stirring in the cold milk until smooth and shiny. Sometimes this mixture looks like it has split. Allow to cool down a bit more and whisk in a little extra cold milk until smooth. Scrape all the mixture into the cooked and cooled pastry shell with a spatula. Shake the tart to even it out and allow to cool for around 1–2 hours until it is at room temperature. Dust with the cocoa powder. Ultimately the pastry should be short and crisp and the filling should be smooth and should cut like butter.

Fruit-filled Mascarpone Tart

This is the ultimate in fast tarts and is great when good berries and soft fruit are available and taste pukka. Slap your mascarpone cream into your cooked and cooled tart shell (see page 214). Smooth off with a palette knife and pile a load of fruit (wash if necessary) on top.

STOCKS, SAUCES,
BITS, BOBS, THIS,
THAT AND THE OTHER

Chicken Stock

Chicken stock is a really useful thing to have in the fridge or freezer and I make a month's supply at a time. I usually buy chicken winglets and thighs, and you can get really cheap carcasses of chicken from your butcher. I've even made chicken stock out of the leftover carcass of a Sunday roast chicken. I just plonk it in a pot and treat it exactly the same as the recipe that I'm going to give you – the stock is perfectly all right, not quite as clear but it tastes lovely.

For 4 litres/7 pints of stock
2kg/4½lb raw chicken carcasses, chopped
½ whole head of garlic, broken up but unpeeled
5 sticks of celery, roughly chopped
2 medium leeks, roughly chopped
2 medium onions, roughly chopped
2 large carrots, roughly chopped
3 bay leaves
3 sprigs of fresh rosemary
5 sprigs of fresh parsley
5 sprigs of fresh thyme
5 whole black peppercorns
6 litres/10½ pints cold water

In a large, deep, thick-bottomed pan place the chicken carcasses, garlic, vegetables, all the herbs and the peppercorns. Add the cold water and bring to the boil, then turn the heat down to a simmer. Continue to simmer for about 3–4 hours, skimming as necessary, then pass the stock through a fine sieve. Allow to cool for about half an hour, then refrigerate. Once the stock is cold it should look clear and slightly amber in colour. At this point I normally divide the stock into small plastic containers and freeze it. It keeps well in the fridge for about 4 days and in the freezer for about 2–3 months.

Fish Stock

Fish stock is another really handy thing to have in the freezer. When you buy fish from your fishmonger, never let him throw the bones away. Keep them, take them home and make some stock out of them. You can always freeze the bones until you need them, but I make the stock and freeze that so it's always to hand if I need it. Some of the best bones for making fish stock are turbot, sole and monkfish – they're full in flavour and very glutinous. Cod, mullet, John Dory, plaice and brill also have good bones, but these are lighter. (I don't usually use any bones from oily fish.)

For 3 litres/5 pints of stock
2kg/4½lb fish bones
2 sticks of celery, roughly chopped
½ fennel bulb, roughly chopped
½ head of garlic, broken up and sliced thinly
2 dried chillies
2 tablespoons olive oil
255ml/9fl oz white wine
3½ litres/6 pints water
juice of 1 lemon
6 sprigs of fresh parsley
3 bay leaves
1 sprig of thyme

Wash the bones thoroughly. If you are using fish heads, remove the gills and the eyes. Roughly chop the bones up and, in a large, deep, thick-bottomed pan, sweat the vegetables, garlic and chillies in the olive oil for a few minutes until they are tender but without any colour. Add the fish bones and continue to sweat for another 3–4 minutes, then add the white wine. Cook for another 2 or 3 minutes and reduce slightly. Add all the cold water and bring to the boil, skimming regularly. Squeeze in your lemon juice and add all the fresh herbs. Simmer for 20 minutes, skimming regularly. (It is important not to cook the fish stock for too long, as it draws a slight bitterness out of the bones and stops it being so clear.) Pass through a sieve and allow to cool. When passed, fish stock can be boiled and reduced to intensify its flavour. It can be stored in the fridge for about 2–3 days, or you can freeze it for 1–2 months. I divide it into small plastic containers and place it in the freezer. A sign of a good stock is when it's tasty, clear and, when cold, sets like jelly.

Vegetable Stock

For roughly 3 litres/5 pints of stock
1 tablespoon olive oil
2 medium onions
2 large carrots, roughly chopped
2 large leeks, roughly chopped
½ head of celery (use the stringy, stalkier bits),
  roughly chopped
½ bulb of fennel, roughly chopped
½ head of garlic, broken up and roughly chopped
4 litres/7 pints water
2 sprigs of thyme
1 sprig of rosemary
3 bay leaves
1 dried chilli
4 peppercorns
2 teaspoons salt

optional: *for a little more interest you can throw*
  in a handful of dried mushrooms

Heat the olive oil in a large, deep, thick-bottomed pan and add all the vegetables and the garlic. Sweat gently without colouring for 5 minutes, until
slightly tender – you can cover with a lid if you want. Add the cold water.
Bring to the boil and skim. Add all the fresh herbs, the chilli, peppercorns and
salt. Simmer this for 2 hours, skimming every now and again. After 2 hours
pass it through a sieve. You can keep the stock in the fridge for up to a week,
or you can freeze it in small containers for about 3–4 months.

Clarifying Stock

When you've made a lovely stock this is a handy recipe for adding and infusing extra flavour, as well as for lifting all the impurities out of the stock and leaving you with a shiny clear broth. This procedure, which is exactly the same as making a French consommé, has, in the past, been made out to be really tough and tricky, but that's complete rubbish.

For 2–3 litres/4–5 pints of stock
3–4 litres/5–7 pints stock
3 egg whites
85g/3oz lean meat or fish, chopped (choose meat
  or fish to correspond with your stock)
1 medium leek, finely chopped
1 stick of celery, very finely chopped
1 ripe plum tomato, finely chopped
1 carrot, peeled and finely chopped
1 good handful of fresh herbs, such as parsley,
  marjoram, oregano

Place your cloudy stock in a large pan. Put the egg whites, the meat or fish and all the vegetables and herbs into a bowl, stir lightly to break up the egg whites, then whisk the mixture well into the stock. Slowly bring to the boil, stirring well for the first few minutes.

Basically what is going to happen is that as the stock comes to the boil, the protein in the egg whites and meat or fish will begin to coagulate, trapping all your finely chopped vegetables and herbs. This acts like a sort of sieve and forms a crust on the top of your stock. The only thing you've got to look out for is not letting it boil – just keep it at a gentle simmer for about half an hour. Generally the bubbles from the simmering stock manage to make a small hole or crack so I just enlarge the hole, carefully, with a ladle. After half an hour, when you've got a good crust and a completely clear stock, allow it to stand for about 10 minutes. Then, using a ladle, carefully pass the clear broth through a fine sieve. If you want to make sure that you don't get any bits in your broth, place a clean tea-towel or napkin in the sieve (or muslin if you can get it), but this is not essential.

You can keep the sieved stock in the fridge for 4 days or freeze it for up to 2 months.

Flavoured Butter

Flavoured butter is really handy if you want to make something quick like garlic bread, or if you want a tasty way to fry fish, meat or vegetables. You can use lots of different flavours. Herbs are good – especially basil, coriander, rosemary, sage or thyme. Or you can use garlic, olives, sun-dried tomatoes, anchovies, chillies and lemon with thyme – whatever you fancy.

Leave some butter at room temperature until soft. Chop your chosen ingredient (it's up to you how much you use – it depends on how dominant a flavour you want) either finely or coarsely. Then just scrunch the ingredient into the butter. With a spatula scrape the mixture on to greaseproof paper, roll up into a sausage shape, fold the sides in and form into an even shape. Refrigerate. This keeps in the freezer for a couple of months.

Clarified Butter

When I make clarified butter I simply put some butter into a pan and put the pan into the oven at the lowest possible setting. After about 45 minutes the butter will have melted and the milk (or the whey) will have sunk to the bottom. Skim off anything that is on the top and pour the clear, clarified golden butter into another container, discarding the whey. Clarified butter has always been popular because it can be heated at very high temperatures while still retaining its buttery taste. Once the butter has cooled down, put it into wraps of greaseproof paper (rolled up like a sausage, pulling in the sides at the end to squeeze into shape), or, quite simply, put it into plastic containers. It can be stored in the fridge for 1–2 weeks or in the freezer for up to 3 months.

You can use clarified butter for frying off meat and fish – it gives it a really clean golden colour.

Mayonnaise

Serves 8
1 large egg yolk
1 tablespoon Dijon mustard
salt to taste
1 tablespoon white wine vinegar
1 tablespoon lemon juice
285ml/½ pint peanut oil
285ml/½ pint olive oil

Mayonnaise can be made in a food processor, by hand with a whisk and a bowl, or in a food mixer. Put the egg yolk, mustard, 3 small pinches of salt, vinegar and lemon juice into a bowl and whisk until the salt has dissolved. Whisking fast, add small drops of the oil bit by bit, so that the eggs can emulsify with it. (If you add it too fast it could split.) When you've added a quarter of the oil it will start to look like mayonnaise, and you can add the oil slightly quicker. If at any point it does split, just pour a tablespoon of boiling water into the mayonnaise and that should re-emulsify it. When you've added all the oil, the mayonnaise should look thick, creamy and slightly yellow. At this point you should check the seasoning.

You can flavour the mayonnaise by adding, for example, chopped herbs, or roasted chopped nuts – basil mayonnaise, dill mayonnaise, roasted almond mayonnaise, for example.

Aïoli

When I make aïoli I use two olive oils: one that is a bit more expensive, a bit more peppery and a bit more gutsy; and a second which is a bit more bland but still nice and mellow. By blending the flavours in this way you achieve an olive oil flavour that isn't too strong or too peppery.

Aïoli is great with cold roast pork. Basil aïoli is good with pink grilled salmon and lemon aïoli works well with crostini in fish broth.

Serves 8
½ small clove of garlic, peeled
1 teaspoon salt
1 large egg yolk
1 teaspoon Dijon mustard
approx. 285ml/½ pint extra virgin olive oil
approx. 285ml/½ pint olive oil
lemon juice, to taste

Smash up the garlic with 1 teaspoon of salt in a pestle and mortar (if you don't have a pestle and mortar you can very finely chop the garlic). Place the egg yolk and mustard in a bowl and whisk. Then start to add your olive oil bit by bit. Once you've blended in a quarter of the olive oil you can start to add the rest in larger amounts. When you've added it all, you can add the garlic and lemon (to taste) and any extra flavours such as basil, fennel tops, dill, chopped roast nuts. To finish just season to taste with salt, freshly ground black pepper and lemon juice.

Bread Sauce

Bread sauce is excellent served with any roast.

Serves 6
1 medium onion, peeled
6 cloves
1 bay leaf
pinch of ground nutmeg
½ teaspoon ground black pepper
1 teaspoon salt
285ml/½ pint milk
115–140g/4–5oz white breadcrumbs
30g/1oz butter
2 tablespoons cream

Put the onion (spiked with cloves), the bay leaf, nutmeg, black pepper, salt and milk into a pan, bring to the boil and simmer for about 5 minutes. Remove from the heat and leave to stand for about 15 minutes. Strain the milk through a sieve, discarding everything else. Bring the milk back to the boil and simmer, stirring in the breadcrumbs bit by bit. It is important to have both fine and coarse breadcrumbs to give an interesting texture. Add the butter and cream and season to taste. If you feel the sauce is too liquid, add some more breadcrumbs, if you feel that it is slightly too thick add a little more milk. Lately, I have been giving my bread sauce a kick with 3–4 good teaspoons of English mustard.

Apple Sauce

Serves 6–8
4 large cooking apples
55g/2oz sugar
juice of 1 lemon
4 cloves
55g/2oz butter

Peel, core and quarter the cooking apples. Place them in a saucepan with the sugar, lemon juice and cloves (you can add a tablespoon of water if you want) and simmer until soft. Remove the cloves, stir in the butter, and either smash everything to a pulp, or semi-squash it so there are still chunks in it – which I quite like.

Mint Sauce

This is the old-fashioned English mint sauce and is good with roast lamb.

Serves 6–8
4 heaped tablespoons freshly chopped mint
1 teaspoon sugar
1 tablespoon hot water
2 pinches of salt
3 tablespoons wine vinegar

Put the mint into a bowl with the sugar and the water. Stir until the sugar is dissolved. Add the salt and the vinegar and allow to stand for at least 30 minutes before using.

Pesto Sauce

Pesto sauce is very widely used. Everyone likes it, and it is very handy for a lot of different dishes, including pasta, grilled and roasted meats, and vegetables. It can be served with anything. These days you can also get purple basil from the supermarkets, so you can make purple pesto which can be used in just as many dishes and makes a nice change. Pesto can be made in a food processor, but it is best made in a pestle and mortar – I don't know why. I suppose it's because pounding and bruising the basil leaves seems to extract more of the beautiful flavours.

Serves 4
¼ clove of garlic, chopped
3 good handfuls of fresh basil, picked
1 handful of lightly roasted pine nuts
1 good handful of grated Parmesan cheese
extra virgin olive oil
salt and freshly ground black pepper
small squeeze of lemon juice (optional)

Put your garlic into a pestle and mortar or a food processor. If you like a strong garlic taste you can add more but I stick to about ¼ clove, which is still quite strong when raw. Pound or pulse this with your fresh basil leaves. Add the cooled, golden roasted pine nuts to the mixture and pound or pulse. Turn out into a bowl and add half the Parmesan. Gently stir this in and add the olive oil, just enough to bind the sauce and get it to the right consistency – semi-wet but firm.

Taste the mixture, and add a little salt and pepper and the rest of the cheese. Add some more oil and taste again. Keep adding a little bit of this and a little bit more of that until you get it right – this is the way to make pesto. There are no real rules, but as long as you make it fresh and use the best ingredients it'll always taste superb. When you taste it for the last time, it might need a squeeze of lemon juice. Lemon juice isn't listed in all recipes but is quite nice, as it brings the fragrance of the basil out.

Salsa Verde

Salsa verde is best made by hand by chopping very finely. Salsa verde keeps well for a day but then starts to deteriorate. It's great with grilled, roasted or boiled meat, fish and vegetables.

Serves 8
1½–2 cloves of garlic, peeled
1 small handful of capers
1 small handful of pickled gherkins (the ones in sweet vinegar)
6 anchovy fillets
2 large handfuls of flat-leaf parsley, picked
1 bunch of fresh basil, picked
1 handful of fresh mint, picked
1 tablespoon Dijon mustard
45ml/3 tablespoons red wine vinegar
approx. 120ml/8 tablespoons your best olive oil
salt and freshly ground black pepper

Finely chop all the ingredients. Put this mixture into a bowl and add the mustard and red wine vinegar. Slowly stir in the olive oil until you achieve the consistency you are looking for and balance the flavours with freshly ground black pepper, and if necessary, sea salt and red wine vinegar.

Chilli and Fennel Salsa

This is lovely with grilled fish or shellfish. It is really nice with baked or grilled salmon or cod fillet – keep the fish in one piece and serve on a large dish, with the sauce spooned over. Allow the fish to cool to room temperature, so that it can marinate and infuse the beautiful flavours. Put the dish in the middle of the table and let everyone help themselves. Serve with boiled potatoes, a nice salad and bread.

Serves 6
4 medium chillies
1 bulb of fennel
juice of 1–2 large lemons
1 handful of fennel tops, if available
approx. 8 tablespoons olive oil
salt and freshly ground black pepper

Deseed and finely chop the chillies. Cut any excess stalks off the top of the fennel, reserving the green feathery leaves. Trim the bottom of the bulb and take away any outside leaves that seem a bit tough. Cut the bulb in half and slice from the root to the top about 2mm apart. Then slice across, 2mm apart, to give you fine dice (you can make it chunkier if you like). Chop the fennel leaves. Put everything into a bowl, squeeze in the juice of 1 lemon (or more, to taste), and stir in the oil. Season with salt and pepper.

Sweet Chilli and Pepper Salsa

Thinly sliced foccacia tastes great with this dip. It is perfect for drinks parties.

Serves 6
2 red peppers
½ red onion, finely chopped
4 medium/large red chillies, deseeded and finely chopped
½ clove of garlic, finely chopped
120ml/8 tablespoons olive oil
1 tablespoon red wine vinegar
1 handful of parsley, finely chopped
1 handful of basil, finely chopped
salt and freshly ground black pepper

Grill the peppers whole, turning at intervals, until the skin is blackened. Place in a bowl while still hot and cover with clingfilm. Leave them to steam (this makes it easier to remove the skin from the peppers). Skin, deseed and finely chop the peppers. Then add the rest of your ingredients and mix well. Taste for seasoning. Leave for 1 hour to let the flavours develop. Check for seasoning before serving.

Chunky Coconut, Tomato, Cucumber and Lime Relish

This is a really nice fresh salad/relish and is very simple to make. It goes especially well with *Fragrant Green Chicken Curry* (see page 122).

Serves 4
16 cherry tomatoes, quartered or roughly chopped
½ fresh coconut, grated or shaved
1 small handful of basil, or coriander, roughly chopped
15cm/6 inches of cucumber, skinned, seeds removed
  and roughly chopped
1 tablespoon olive oil
salt and freshly ground black pepper
juice of 1–2 limes
1 thinly sliced red chilli (optional)

Put the tomatoes, coconut, basil, cucumber and chilli, if using, into a bowl and toss. Just before serving, toss in the olive oil, salt, pepper and lime juice to taste.

Basic Tomato Sauce

This sauce can be frozen for a couple of months, or refrigerated for up to a week, and is the basis of a lot of dishes.

Serves 6–8
1 large clove of garlic, finely chopped
2 tablespoons olive oil
1 small dried red chilli, crumbled
2 teaspoons dried oregano
3 × 400g/14oz tins of Italian plum tomatoes
1 tablespoon red wine vinegar
1 handful of basil or marjoram (or both), roughly chopped
salt and freshly ground black pepper
2–3 tablespoons extra virgin olive oil

In a thick-bottomed pan gently fry the garlic with the olive oil, then add the chilli, oregano and tomatoes. Mix gently, but do not break up the tomatoes as this will release the pips, which will make the sauce slightly bitter – by leaving the tomatoes whole and letting the mixture cook slowly you'll get a nice sweet sauce. (You can remove the pips from the tomatoes if you want, but I don't bother.) Bring to the boil and simmer gently for 1 hour. Add the vinegar, then stir and chop up the tomatoes in the sauce. Now add your fresh basil or marjoram (or both), season well to taste, and add 2–3 tablespoons of your best extra virgin olive oil.

Pickled Chillies

Pickled chillies are absolutely superb. They are brilliant because they can just sit in the fridge waiting to be used. I particularly like to use them in stir-frying or in broths or to eat them just as they are with some cheese and bread. They are really good, and you should try them.

600g/1lb 5oz medium green chillies
15 black peppercorns
5 bay leaves
2 tablespoons coriander seeds
5 teaspoons salt
6 heaped tablespoons caster sugar
1 litre/1¾ pints white wine vinegar or rice vinegar

For this recipe you must buy perfect green chillies without any blemishes (you can use red chillies but they will be slightly hotter). Carefully score from the stalk end to the tip on one side only and remove the seeds (use the handle of a teaspoon for this). Pour boiling water over the chillies, let them sit for 5 minutes, then drain. This will get rid of most of the seeds left behind. Next put your black peppercorns, bay leaves, coriander, chillies and salt into a large jar or other airtight container. Put the sugar and the vinegar into a pan and heat until the sugar is fully dissolved. When this is quite hot, but not boiling, pour it into the jar with the chillies. Allow it to cool down and then put the lid on, put into the fridge and leave for a minimum of 2 weeks before using. They will keep in the fridge for at least 4 months.

Page numbers in bold denote illustration

THANKS

To my mum and dad for giving me a great childhood and chances. And to Jules, my fiancée, for putting up with me and giving me a slap and tickle when need be.

To Rose Gray and Ruthie Rogers for their time, encouragement and support. To Gennaro Contaldo for taking me under his wing and giving me some of the real feel, love and spirit for earthy Italian food. Ya bastard! To Paul and Anna for their encouragement and ideas at the start. To Willo for selling me a dodgy scooter. To Bender the Aussie for being a great laugh, friend, helping hand and a damn fine cook (and for pulling moonies unconditionally!). To the Guth Boys Inc. Arthur, Ben Number 2, Ashley, Theo, Peter, Gary and Danie.

To Mark Phillips Ansell for his tuition and gags in the early years, and everyone else at the Cricketers in Clavering. To Tell Tale, Tesco for the bits researching the rest of the supermarkets.

To Jean Cazals and David Eustace for their amazing photographs and for making hectic days a laugh. To Michael Joseph/Penguin for putting as much into this book as I have: Tom Weldon, Johnny Boy Hamilton, Nick 'Zeus' Wilson, lovely Lindsey Jordan, Nici Stanley and James Holland. Cheers.

To Optomen Television and everyone involved in making the programme: Pat Llewellyn, Peter Gillbe, Corinne Field, pukka Polly, little Lucy and the rest of the team. Thanks for making my life hell for three months! Lots of love. And to Ginny Alcock and Kate Habershom, the food stylists, for all their help and hard work.

I'd like to thank a few of London's best suppliers who, apart from giving great service, give that little bit more with a personal touch. Thank you. The 4 dons are:

Lovely Patricia at La Fromagerie, 30 Highbury Park, London N5 2AA (the best cheese shop in England). Tel: 0171 359 7440.

Brian Randalls Butchers, 113 Wandsworth Bridge Road, London SW6 2TE. Tel: 0171 736 3426.

Barry the Boy, Portobello Road Market.

Rushton at George Allans Vegetables, Unit 12–14, C Block, New Covent Garden Market. Tel: 0171 720 3485.